Your One-Stop Guide to
Patron Saints

Your One-Stop Guide to Patron Saints

CATHERINE M. ODELL

CHARIS

SERVANT PUBLICATIONS
ANN ARBOR, MICHIGAN

Charis Books is an imprint of Servant Publications especially designed to
serve Roman Catholics.

Servant Publications
P.O. Box 8617
Ann Arbor, MI 48107

Cover design by Hile Illustration and Design–Ann Arbor, Michigan

01 02 03 04 10 9 8 7 6 5 4 3 2 1

Printed in the United States of America
ISBN 1-56955-302-5

LIBRARY OF CONGRESS CATALOGING-IN-PUBLICATION DATA

Odell, Catherine
    Your one-stop guide to patron saints / Catherine Odell.
        p. cm.
    Includes index.
    ISBN 1-56955-302-5 (alk. paper)
     1. Christian patron saints. I. Title.
    BX4656.5 .O34 2001
    282'.092'2—dc21

                                                     2001003870

Dedication

For my son,
Luke Samuel,
and for my daughter,
Juliana Marie.

Contents

Introduction: Who Are These Patron Saints? 9

Chapter 1
Patron Saints of Church Life and Faith 15

Chapter 2
Patron Saints of Family Life and Home 39

Chapter 3
Patron Saints of Work Life and Occupations 57

Chapter 4
Patron Saints of Those With Illnesses or Special Needs 95

Chapter 5
Patron Saints of Nations and Continents 111

Indices of Patron Saints
Index by Patron Saint's Name 133
Index by Patronage of Work, Association, Institution,
Need, or Place 141

Bibliography 153

Who Are These Patron Saints?

Patron saints are saints venerated as special protectors or inter-cessors. Individual men and women, professions, cities, nations, continents, and people facing particular problems may all have a patron saint. Catholics take a saint's name at baptism and thereby receive that saint as a patron saint. The assignment of patron saints in those other categories, however, has been a wonderful but gloriously haphazard venture for the last two thousand years.

Some professions have patron saints, while others don't. Many nations have a patron saint "on call," but not all do. Patron saints have been linked to special needs, to ailments, and to just about every job under the sun. And the list is fairly timely. St. Isidore of Seville, a bishop seen as a walking library in seventh-century Spain, has been recently drafted by many Catholics as the patron saint of computer users and the Internet.

Sometimes a saint's patronage can be clearly understood. St. Blase, a fourth-century martyr who healed a child choking on a fish bone, seems a nifty fit for the patron saint of throat ailments. St. Camillus de Lellis, a one-time compulsive gambler, makes a believable patron saint for gambling addicts.

But in other cases, the connection between a saint and the patronage is more difficult to uncover, more circumstantial, or even funny. The seventeenth-century Italian mystic St. Joseph of Cupertino apparently won the job as patron saint of astronauts and pilots because his spiritual gifts included flying in ecstasy to the ceiling of his Franciscan monastery.

Few patron saints have been officially designated by the Church. Among the hundreds of patron saints, there are less than sixty "official" patron saints. Among the latest named by the Church was St. Thomas More, the martyred champion of political conscience who was beheaded at the command of King Henry VIII of England in 1535.

In October of 2000, Pope John Paul II named Thomas More the "patron saint of politicians." That's a daunting, demanding assignment, even if Thomas' new role put him in charge of American politicians alone! But politicians all over the world?

In 1999, the Holy Father thoughtfully added three women as patron saints of Europe. Two charismatic, beautiful, and holy fourteenth-century women—Sts. Catherine of Siena and Bridget of Sweden—joined a brilliant twentieth-century Jewish Carmelite martyr, St. Edith Stein (officially, St. Teresa Benedicta of the Cross). John Paul II matched these new patrons with three previously named male patrons for Europe. St. Benedict, the sixth-century father of Western monasticism, had already been interceding for the continent along with Sts. Cyril and Methodius, ninth-century missionaries to Macedonia, Greece, Russia, and Moravia.

By and large, however, the linkage of individual saints to a cause, a region, or an ailment has come about through popular, local interest. People of faith are strengthened by heroes of faith. They long for role models, faith-filled pioneers who followed the Savior in their own way in their own day. Whenever a saintly role model has attracted enough attention, he or she typically has become a de facto patron saint.

Truthfully, the attraction to all saints and their stories has engaged Christians from the first Christian centuries. Even non-believers have recognized the persuasive power in their example. "Give me ten men like St. Francis of Assisi," Nikolai Lenin once conceded, "and I will change the world."

Saints are Christian believers who have reached the reward of life in heaven with God. In the early history of the Church, many felt that only martyrs—those who gave their lives as Jesus did—could be confidently viewed as saints. But gradually it was understood that a person who gave his or her life for God in service might be just as truly a saint.

Long before formal canonizations began in the tenth century, Christians honored other Christians who died after holy lives. These saintly men and women were chosen as models by popular acclaim. In fact, honoring prophets and holy people with shrines was a Jewish practice as well. Christian patterns of honoring saints built on these Jewish traditions.

Our connection with all saints is fundamentally rooted in our creed. It has solid theological roots. We call this connection "the communion of saints." As Pope Paul VI wrote: "We believe in the communion of all the faithful of Christ, those who are pilgrims on earth, the dead who are being purified, and the blessed in heaven, all together forming one Church; and we believe that in this communion, the merciful love of God and his saints is always [attentive] to our prayers."*

Today, we are those pilgrims on earth. But our connection with God, with heaven, and with heaven's blessed community has been better understood and accepted in the past. In our own day, skepticism concerning spiritual realities is more prevalent and

---

*Pope Paul VI, *Creed of the People of God*, June 30, 1968.

even fashionable. If science can't measure, clone, dissect, atom-ize, or chemically analyze any given thing, some assume that it isn't real.

Nevertheless, each saint is real. The canonized and uncanon-ized stand in heaven awestruck, overjoyed, and endlessly ful-filled by the vision of God. Each saint lives within the mystery of divine love. In heaven as on earth, love means being selflessly connected with another.

So even after death, the saints seek to be connected with us for the sake of love. As the *Catechism of the Catholic Church* tells us, "the saints contemplate God, praise him and constantly care for those whom they have left on earth. When they entered into the joy of their Master, they were 'put in charge of many things.'... We can and should ask them to intercede for us and for the whole world" (*CCC* 2683).

We know that some saints looked forward to this eternity of earthly assignments. Before she died at twenty-four in her con-vent in northeastern France in 1879, St. Thérèse of Lisieux gasped, "I want to spend my heaven doing good on earth."

Six centuries earlier, fifty-one-year-old St. Dominic had tried to ease the pain of his parting as his tearful brothers gathered around him. He was stretched out in a borrowed habit, dying on a borrowed bed. "Do not weep," he told them, "for I shall be more useful to you after my death, and I shall help then more effectively than during my life."

The patronage of saints—their willing connection with us—can't be proven scientifically. Nor can it be seen as a major article of our Catholic faith. But it's real. It's there for those who wish to see the communion of saints in the glorious, expansive, and timeless way in which the Church presents it.

The late Cardinal John O'Connor of New York once wrote

with awe about his mother's deep devotion to St. Rita of Cascia. St. Rita was a fifteenth-century Italian wife and mother who became—by popular assignment—a patron saint of infertile couples, an intercessor for those in unhappy marriages and those in desperate situations!

"My mother was very big on St. Rita of Cascia. And why not?" Cardinal O'Connor once wrote. "My mother lost her sight after my birth and recovered it—she believed until her dying day—through the intercession of St. Rita of Cascia. What was it to my mother that week after week for the rest of her life she had to take two trolley cars and a bus both ways to make the novena at St. Rita's Church in Philadelphia? Do you think that didn't make an impression on me?"*

Mrs. O'Connor and others in her good company down through the centuries ask patron saints to join with them in prayer. Despite an old and persistent misunderstanding, Catholics do not worship the saints—even the Blessed Virgin Mary, who is the preeminent patron saint, especially of places. God alone is the worthy recipient of our worship and adoration.

Nevertheless, the saints are worthy of our honor as our spiritual heroes, role models, and family members. These heavenly friends delight in having us ask them to pray for us, just as our friends on earth gladly respond when we ask them for their prayers.

The grand and engaging company of the patron saints is a loving, fascinating, and generous community. May you find among them a special kinship, an enduring friendship, a patron in your need.

---

*Cardinal John J. O'Connor, "Saints and Then Some," *Catholic Heritage,* November/December 1991, 13.

Chapter One

Patron Saints of Church Life and Faith

Altar Servers
St. John Berchmans (1599–1621), Belgium
Like most parents of large families, John's mother and father were amazed at the differences among their five children. John had a wonderful memory and was amazingly devout. At age seven, this shoemaker's son would rise to serve the morning Masses at the church in Diest. When John's mother became very ill, he spent hours at her bedside each day. There was no trace of self-righteous superiority in John. He simply had an understanding of goodness and a great attraction to it.

At age seventeen, John joined the Jesuits and went to Rome. Very good at languages, John dreamed of teaching the faith to migrants. In seminary, John shone academically but even more in his remarkable virtues. His faithfulness to obedience even in little things was echoed two centuries later in the spirituality of St. Thérèse of Lisieux. He died suddenly from a high fever at age twenty-two. Canonized: 1888. Feast: November 26.

Bishops
St. Patrick (389–461), Ireland
Patrick spent his childhood along the western coast of Britain or Scotland. At age sixteen, he was kidnapped and taken to Ireland as a slave. There the lonely Patrick herded and learned to pray.

After six years he escaped, then went to Gaul and became a priest and monk. Later Patrick had a powerful dream and felt a call to return to Ireland.

As a bishop, Patrick dedicated himself completely to spreading the gospel throughout Ireland. At Tara, he confronted a Druid priest on Holy Saturday and established his credibility with the pagan tribes. Beloved by his people, Patrick was linked to many miracles before and after his death at Saul, Downpatrick. Legends claim that Patrick drove the snakes from Ireland and taught the Trinity while holding a three-leaf clover. Canonized: By popular acclaim. Feast: March 17.

Canon Lawyers
St. Raymond of Peñafort (1175–1275), Spain

Few saints have lived a hundred years! Apparently, God needed Raymond's special gifts for a long time. Born to a noble family in Spain, Raymond was a relative of Aragon's king. Intelligent as well as wealthy, Raymond finished studies at a very young age.

Throughout childhood he maintained a deep devotion to Mary. He became a priest, then a lawyer, and then a university professor. In 1218, Raymond joined the Jesuits. In 1230, he went to Rome at the pope's request. It was there that Raymond did his most important work for the Church. He rewrote and indexed canon laws, and the Church made use of this work until 1917.

The pope tried to reward Raymond by making him an archbishop. But Raymond preferred to return to Spain and parish work. Back home, Raymond founded language schools for missionaries and worked with St. Thomas Aquinas to explain the faith for nonbelievers. Canonized: 1601. Feast: January 7.

Catechists
St. Robert Bellarmine (1542–1621), Italy

In a large family, it's easier to learn generosity. But Robert, the third of ten children, was also influenced by his mother's dedication to prayer, almsgiving, and fasting. At age eighteen, he joined the new Jesuit order. Well prepared, Robert had studied Scripture and Church history for years. This brilliant student later became a brilliant teacher.

The Protestant Reformation had begun. At age twenty-eight, Robert became director or "chair" of Controversial Theology at the Roman College. There was plenty to do, defending and teaching the faith. He taught theology to university students, but he also taught catechism to children. He wrote catechisms and many other works.

At age fifty-six, Robert became a cardinal. He could have lived elegantly in the Vatican, but Cardinal Bellarmine gave everything away. Once, he gave expensive wall tapestries to clothe the poor. "The walls won't catch cold," he said. Canonized: 1930. Named Doctor of the Church: 1931. Feast: September 17.

Catholic Action
St. Francis of Assisi (1182–1226), Italy

Everyone in Assisi thought that the slender, fun-loving Francisco would become a wealthy textile merchant, just like his father. But by age twenty, Francisco was a sick, imprisoned soldier. Suddenly, Francis saw life differently. He wanted to work for Christ.

Renouncing his inheritance, he began to preach the gospel and beg for a living. Joined by others, Francis founded the Franciscans in 1209. His happiness and joy in God's love overflowed into his prayers and his love of animals and all of God's creation.

Francis also put his love and faith to work. He preached to the birds and to the fish. At Gubbio, he once befriended and tamed a wolf that threatened the village. In 1224, Francis, weakened and ill, retreated from active leadership of the order. He received the stigmata, the wounds of Christ, and died quietly in 1226. Canonized: 1228, only two years after his death. Feast: October 4.

Catholic Press
St. Francis de Sales (1567–1622), Savoy

Born in Savoy, Francis led a privileged life and tried to please his wealthy father. The oldest of thirteen and the eldest son, Francis became a lawyer. But his heart belonged to God, and in 1593, he became a priest.

Francis was quickly sent to Geneva to bring Calvinists back to the Catholic faith. He was an extremely persuasive preacher, but there was great resistance to Catholics. Calvinists tried to assassinate him more than once. Finally, Francis began writing and distributing a weekly Catholic newsletter. It reached thousands. Soon, he won most of the people back and became Geneva's bishop.

With St. Jane Frances de Chantal, Francis founded the Visitation Sisters. He wrote several spiritual classics, including *Introduction to the Devout Life*. "Ask for nothing, refuse nothing," was his motto. Overworked, he collapsed, lost his hearing, and died of a cerebral hemorrhage at age fifty-five. Canonized: 1655. Named Doctor of the Church: 1877. Feast: January 24.

Catholic Schools
St. Thomas Aquinas (c.1225–74), Italy

Thomas was only five when his school days began. The youngest Aquinas son went to Monte Cassino, a Benedictine abbey. Everyone saw that Thomas was very bright and big.

At age fourteen, Thomas was sent to the University of Naples and read the works of Blessed Jordan of Saxony, a Dominican. Jordan's ideas captured Thomas. His family opposed his attraction to the Dominicans, but finally, there was nothing they could do. This strong-willed, strapping Thomas had a mind of his own.

And what a mind! Because he was shy, some students dubbed Thomas "the dumb ox." After ordination, this "dumb ox" became the most exciting philosophy teacher at the University of Paris. He wrote the *Summa Theologica*, a brilliant philosophical examination of the faith. And yet before his death, Thomas saw that all this knowledge couldn't compare to personally knowing God. Canonized: 1323. Named Doctor of the Church: 1567. Feast: January 28.

Chaplains, Military Chaplains
St. John Capistran (1386–1456), Italy

John's role as a chaplain for a crusade against the Turks led to his patronage for chaplains. But this Franciscan friar had already had a half-dozen other careers: lawyer, governor of Perugia, brilliant theologian, phenomenal preacher, diplomat for the king of France and the pope, minister of healing. He was all of these though he had initially chosen marriage and a law career.

Like St. Francis, John reassessed his life during a wartime imprisonment. Since his marriage wasn't yet consummated, he applied for an annulment and went to study theology with St.

Bernardine of Siena. After ordination, John traveled up and down the Italian peninsula, preaching to gigantic crowds. In Brescia, he once drew 126,000 people!

Like his mentor, Bernardine, John was very devoted to the Holy Name of Jesus. While serving the pope as apostolic nuncio, he died in Austria at age seventy. Canonized: 1724. Named patron of chaplains: 1984. Memorial: March 28.

Charitable Organizations
St. Vincent de Paul (1581–1660), France

"*Monsieur* Vincent," as the young priest called himself, never planned to devote himself to the poor. In fact, as he later admitted, he wanted a "comfortable" priestly assignment. The de Pauls were peasants in Gascony. As a boy, Vincent tended his father's sheep and pigs. Vincent didn't resent his childhood deprivations. He simply wanted to better himself—until Providence intervened.

It happened during a deathbed visit to a despairing peasant. Vincent was the spiritual director for the wealthy de Gondis. The young priest comforted the dying patient, but thought his own heart would break. From that day, he worked to organize Church efforts for the poor.

In Paris, he organized a lay group called the "Ladies of Charity." Later, with Louise de Marillac, also a future saint, he founded the Daughters of Charity. Until his death at age seventy-nine, he wore patched clothing and rose at four o'clock each morning to pray. Canonized: 1737. Feast: September 27.

The Church
St. Joseph (first century), Galilee

Joseph was a descendant of King David's family. Scripture texts in Matthew 1-2 and Luke 1-2 sketch the portrait of a faithful, obedient man of God and a trustworthy father and protector. Despite earlier misgivings about Mary's pregnancy, Joseph heard God and married her. He understood that her Child was divine. Thus Joseph became the foster father and protector of Jesus.

Joseph acted when he needed to. He took his family to Egypt to protect Jesus from Herod. Later, they settled in sleepy Nazareth. There, Joseph taught Jesus carpentry and died before the Lord's public life began. With Mary and Jesus tearfully tending him, faithful Joseph had a happy death. Canonized: By popular acclaim. Feasts: March 19; May 1 as patron saint of workers.

Confessors
St. Alphonsus Liguori (1696–1787), Italy

As the firstborn of a large Neapolitan noble family, Alphonsus knew about family expectations. He became a lawyer at his father's insistence. But at twenty-seven, he abandoned law and a marriage planned for him. Instead, he became a priest, and soon was living out a vow never to waste a moment.

In Naples, Alphonsus founded "Evening Chapels" for restless young people. In 1732, he launched the Redemptorists to help the poor. There were many agonizing setbacks for the order. Meanwhile, he wrote 111 books and became a bishop.

For most of his ninety-one years, Alphonsus suffered from asthma and severe rheumatism. He could barely lift his head off his chest. A compassionate but firm confessor, he once summoned a worldly priest. Alphonsus had laid a crucifix across the threshold of the room. "Be sure to trample it," he told the priest. "It wouldn't be the first time." Canonized: 1839. Named Doctor of the Church: 1871. Memorial: August 1.

Converts
St. Charles Lwanga (c. 1864–86), Uganda

"I have power to kill you," a Roman judge told an early Church martyr. "But I have power to be killed," the martyr answered. That same faith strengthened convert Charles Lwanga and twenty-one other Ugandan Christians when they faced death in 1886.

Lwanga and the others were new Christian converts. Lwanga was also the chief of royal pages at the court of a dissolute pedophile, King Mwanga. Mwanga often seduced boys serving him and had developed a smoldering hatred for Christians. They dared to challenge him!

When Charles Lwanga heard the drums announcing their execution, he gathered the Christians to strengthen them. On June 3, twenty-two Christians were thrown onto a blazing fire to die. Lwanga was thrown on a slow-burning fire to extend his agonies. *"Katonda, Katonda"* ("O my God"), Lwanga prayed as he died. Canonized with his companions: 1964. Feast: June 3.

Deacons
St. Stephen, Martyr (died c. 33), Judea

Was Stephen a Greek or a Jew from Jerusalem? So much we might have known about him was lost to us when he died near the Damascus Gate, where he was stoned. But we do know that he was the first Christian martyr and one of the first seven deacons of the Church. He gave everything to serve the Church and Christ.

Stephen and others were assigned to care especially for the widows and dependents of Greek converts. The apostles had heard complaints that only Hebrew widows were getting help. Stephen carried out his responsibilities with great devotion, the Acts of the Apostles reports. He also had a ministry of healing.

Stephen was thrown down outside the city and stoned. His last prayer was, "Lord Jesus, receive my spirit." The Church of Jerusalem retrieved Stephen's body and mourned him deeply. Canonized: By popular acclaim in the first century. Feast: December 26.

Doubters
St. Thomas the Apostle (first century), Galilee
Poor Thomas! The Gospel story of his shocking doubts about the risen Jesus is so familiar. Thomas, one of the twelve apostles, was absent when the resurrected Lord first appeared (see Jn 20:24-31). On the second visit, however, Thomas was present. He recognized and adored Jesus with a new confession of faith: "My Lord and my God!"

Legends suggest that Thomas later preached the gospel in India, while some old stories say he went to Persia. Others tell us that Thomas was martyred in India. Some accounts say his relics were then returned to Edessa, in what is now Turkey.

Thomas is seen as a builder since he built so many church communities during his journeys. His early doubts were left behind. A person of deep faith, according to Catholic writer G.K. Chesterton, "cannot help believing." The example of Thomas should encourage many who suffer doubts. Canonized: By popular acclaim. Feast: July 3.

Ecumenists
Sts. Cyril (826–69) and Methodius (815–85), Greece

Born in Thessalonica, these dynamic brothers were remembered for a thousand years by Central Europeans, especially the Czechs, Croats, Serbs, and Bulgars. They were successful in their careers—teaching and government—before deciding to become priests. Though twelve years apart in age, they were inseparable after their ordination.

In 863, the two became missionaries in Moravia, in present-day Czechoslovakia. They were highly successful in spreading the gospel. Cyril and Methodius had learned the native language and showed respect and tolerance for all. Under their influence, Christianity began to flower in Moravia.

In 869, the two went back to Rome, where Cyril died. The pope consecrated the grieving Methodius as a bishop and sent him back. This time, however, German bishops, angry about his permission to celebrate the liturgy in Slavonic, imprisoned him. But Methodius endured and even translated the Bible into Slavonic, using the alphabet Cyril had developed. Canonized together: 1880. Feast: February 14.

Eucharistic Congresses and Movements
St. Paschal Baylon (1540–92), Spain

Paschal's name is linked to his birth on Pentecost. In Spain, Pentecost was called "the Pasch (or Passover) of the Holy Spirit." The boy's parents were devout peasants who encouraged his early and lasting devotion to the Eucharist.

As a shepherd boy, Paschal mixed with other shepherds, and his good Christian example didn't go unnoticed. Young people were impressed and began to imitate him. He entered religious life as a lay Franciscan brother of the Alcantarine reform.

Because of his minimal education, Paschal became a cook and doorkeeper. And yet there was a depth to his spirituality that even scholars could envy. Once during a trip through France, Paschal, the unschooled cook, successfully debated the real presence of Christ in the Eucharist with a Calvinist preacher. The Protestant crowd almost killed him, but Paschal escaped. A counselor to people of all social stations, he was gentle, loving to the poor, and patient. Canonized: 1690. Feast: May 17.

First Communicants
St. Tarsicius (third or fourth century), Rome
First Communion Day is very special. The First Communicant—usually a young boy or girl—receives the Body and Blood of Christ for the first time. We learn to value the Eucharist even more when we discover that receiving or giving the Eucharist has often been dangerous for Christians.

Tarsicius was probably a deacon in Rome during the era of Christian persecutions. One day, he was carrying the Eucharist to others when he was stopped by Roman authorities. As he defended the sacrament of Christ's Body, Tarsicius was beaten and killed.

It is said that when the bloodied, broken body of the saint was turned over, the Eucharist he'd carried had miraculously disappeared. Tarsicius was buried in the Catacombs of St. Callistus near Rome. Later, Pope Damasus honored the martyr with a poem inscribed at his tomb. Canonized: By popular acclaim. Feast: August 15.

Foreign Missions
St. Thérèse of Lisieux (1873–97), France

Pretty, smart, strong-willed little Thérèse Martin was the four-year-old "baby of the family" when her mother died. Thérèse grieved again when her older sister Pauline left to be a Carmelite nun. But at age fifteen, Thérèse joined the Carmelites.

For nine years, she lived in the cold, drafty convent at Lisieux. She found a way to do every task for Christ. In her autobiography, *The Story of a Soul*, she called this approach her "Little Way." When invited to join the missions in Vietnam, she refused, though being a missionary had been her dream. The twenty-four-year-old knew she had tuberculosis and was dying.

Almost unknown during her lifetime, Thérèse became a twentieth-century hero. She promised to "let fall a shower of roses" after her death. "I shall come back to earth," she said, "to teach others to love." Canonized: 1925. Named patron saint of foreign missions: 1927; named Doctor of the Church: 1997. Feast: October 1.

Friendship
St. John the Apostle (died c. 100), Galilee

The dying Jesus entrusted his mother Mary to John. Clearly, Jesus saw John as a very close friend. That friendship began while John and his older brother James were still fishermen. These sons of Zebedee were well known in Galilee.

John may have been a favorite for Jesus because, at age twenty, he was much younger than the other apostles. John and James were called the "Sons of Thunder" (see Mk 3:17), and may have been highly emotional. But John was also very loving and kind.

The only apostle not martyred, John left Jerusalem after his brother James was beheaded. At Ephesus in Asia Minor, John wrote his Gospel, epistles, and the Apocalypse. When John was too old and tired to preach, St. Jerome later wrote, he would simply tell people: "Love one another.... If you keep this command of the Lord, it is enough." Also called "the Evangelist," "the Beloved," "the Divine." Canonized: By popular acclaim. Feast: December 27.

Hermits
St. Anthony the Great (251–356), Egypt

Living a hermit's life is a special calling. Even as a boy in Egypt, Anthony liked to be solitary. At age twenty, his parents died, leaving their property to Anthony and his younger sister. Soon after that, Anthony heard the gospel words about giving what you have to the poor. Instantly, he felt called. He provided for his sister, gave the remaining money away, and retreated to the desert.

In a desert cave, Anthony conquered great temptations and grew strong. His reputation for holiness also grew, and devotees pursued him. For twenty years, he blocked his doorway with stones and lived in total seclusion. But when anxious visitors pulled down the barricade, he welcomed them.

Anthony's leadership was needed to found desert hermitages and defend persecuted Christians in Alexandria. His long, holy life brought him into contact with many people, including Emperor Constantine. Like John the Baptist, Anthony joyfully lived on dates, bread, and water. Canonized: By popular acclaim. Feast: January 17.

Interracial Justice and Ministry
St. Martin de Porres (1579–1639), Peru

Children of a Spanish knight and a former slave of African descent, Martin and his sister were rejected by their father because of their color. Smart and talented, Martin was wounded by his father's attitude. Martin knew, however, that his heavenly Father loved him unconditionally.

Though well trained as a barber and doctor, Martin became a simple Dominican brother. He slept little and cared for the sick, the poor, the hungry, and the slaves of Lima. With donations, he founded an orphanage for children of all races.

Martin's prayers were also linked to many healings. He even worked wonders with animals. Once, he calmed a raging bull in the city plaza. He also fed mice and rats each day in the Dominican monastery garden. Martin had banished them from the sacristy, where the pesky rodents had chewed and damaged vestments. Canonized: 1962. Feast: November 3.

Lectors
St. Sabas (died 372), Romania

In Bucharest, Sabas was a gifted lector and cantor. His was an important role in the days when not everyone could read. Sabas served with a priest named Sansala.

Reading the Scriptures each day at Mass brought him into a dangerous limelight. A Gothic ruler in the vicinity had set out to persecute and eradicate every Christian he could find. Sabas was arrested once and then released because he didn't seem important enough.

Imprisoned again, Sabas was beaten but refused to cooperate. Using his formidable orator's skills, he renounced his captors and their commanders. When he refused to eat meat sacrificed to pagan gods, an order for his execution was given. According to a witness, he was tied to a pole and then drowned in a river. Fifty other Christians were martyred as well. Sabas is a favorite saint in the Eastern Church. Canonized: By popular acclaim. Feast: April 12.

Missions Among People of African Descent
St. Peter Claver (1580–1654), Spain

Peter had been a shy, nervous seminarian. The son of a farmer, he feared that he wasn't worthy of the priesthood. Nonetheless, the desire to serve God as a Jesuit missionary sustained him.

In 1610, the thirty-year-old went to Cartagena in Colombia. There, Peter was soon ordained and put to work. For forty-four years, he served shackled, filthy, hungry, terrified slaves arriving from Africa.

As best he could, Peter learned their languages and tried to comfort them. While the slaves waited to be sold, Peter taught them that God loved them. He taught about Christianity, a religion of hope. "I am the slave of the Negroes forever," he assured them.

Many in Cartagena ridiculed and persecuted Peter because he treated slaves as human beings. But through it all, Father Peter endured. During his last years, he was neglected while paralyzed and in pain. Canonized: 1888. Named patron of missions among people of African descent in 1896. Feast: September 9.

Monks
St. Benedict of Nursia (c. 480–547), Italy

In his youth, Benedict was offended by Rome, the city some saw as the center of the universe. Rome was no longer noble and great, Benedict believed. To find peace, Benedict became a hermit near Subiaco, Italy.

Soon, some monks asked him to become their abbot. Benedict agreed but instituted strict discipline. Several monks greatly resented this and almost poisoned him!

Benedict left and founded twelve new monasteries. Many men became monks, drawn by stories about Benedict's miracles and sanctity. He wrote a rule to guide his monasteries. The day was divided into periods for work and prayer. *Laborare est orare*—"To work is to pray"—became their motto.

Benedict's twin sister, Scholastica, was a nun who lived nearby and visited him each year. The sixty-three-year-old father of Western Monasticism died standing up, supported by his monks. Canonized: By popular acclaim. Feast: July 11.

Mystics
St. John of the Cross (1542–91), Spain
The youngest son of a Toledo silk weaver, John was a good student, but he was also committed to prayer and fasting. John joined the Carmelites at Medina and asked to follow its original, strict regulations. In 1567, he met fifty-two-year-old St. Teresa of Avila, who was reforming Carmelite convents. Kindred spirits right from the start, the two began to work in tandem.

John soon founded the first reformed house for men. Angered at his audacity, the Carmelite superior imprisoned and tortured him for nearly a year. In his dark cell, John couldn't even stand upright. Though he was beaten routinely and given only bread and water, his spirit found deeper joy in visions of God.

John began writing beautiful theology and poetry about the spiritual life. Later, he wrote the spiritual classics *The Dark Night of the Soul* and *Ascent of Mount Carmel.* Canonized: 1726. Named Doctor of the Church: 1926. Feast: December 14.

Nuns
St. Brigid (or Bride or Briege) (451–525), Ireland

Brigid was eleven when St. Patrick died in Downpatrick. Patrick had baptized her at Faughart. Little is known about Brigid, but in Ireland, legends come to the rescue when facts are scarce.

It seems certain that the lovely Brigid entered religious life at age seventeen. With seven other virgins, she built and founded a convent near a large oak tree at Kildare. She later added a school of art and illumination. Kildare thus became a religious and cultural center.

The common people loved Brigid for her charity. "Everything that Brigid would ask of the Lord was granted at once," reported the Book of Lismore, "for this was her desire to satisfy the poor, to drive out every hardship, to spare every miserable man." Brigid was abbess of the first women's religious community in Ireland and had unique influence for a woman of that time. Her bones were later reburied with Patrick's. Canonized: By popular acclaim. Feast: February 1.

The Papacy
St. Peter the Apostle (died c. 67), Galilee

"You are Peter," Jesus told a Galilean named Simon, "and upon this rock, I will build my church." The name *Peter* means "rock." Jesus built his Church on an impetuous and bossy fisherman.

But Peter had a quality that Jesus needed: Peter loved God with undying selflessness. It was Peter who stepped out of the boat to walk on the water towards his Master. Peter couldn't help blurting out, "You are the Christ, the Son of the living God!" (Mt 16:16). This deep and faithful love was what Jesus wanted in Peter's successors—the popes.

After Pentecost, Peter did become a strong rock. He traveled through Asia Minor and finally settled in Rome. There he was crucified upside down during the Emperor Nero's reign. Peter is reportedly buried below the main altar of St. Peter's Basilica in Rome. Canonized: By popular acclaim. Feasts: Sts. Peter and Paul: June 29; St. Peter's Chair: February 22.

Parish Missions
St. Leonard of Port Maurice (1676–1751), Italy

A "superstar" of preachers? If anyone fit the description in seventeenth-century Italy, it was Friar Leonard. From his childhood he was focused on sharing God's Word. He studied theology with the Jesuits but joined the *Riformella* Franciscans.

Just before Leonard left for the missions in China, he fell ill. When he recovered, he began preaching near his hometown, Porto Maurice. The people loved him! Leonard continued, praying and fasting to protect himself from pride.

Crowds assembled outside because no churches could accommodate them. Up and down the Italian peninsula Leonard and other parish preachers traveled. He encouraged devotion to the Sacred Heart, perpetual adoration of the Blessed Sacrament, and the stations of the cross. His sermons and ascetic writings filled volumes.

Father Leonard built over 550 stations of the cross. Though his enthusiasm never slowed, his body did. He died in Rome at age seventy-five. Canonized: 1867. Named patron of parish missions: 1923. Feast: November 26.

Pilgrims and Pilgrimages
St. James the Greater (died c. 44), Galilee

The elder son of Zebedee was a fisherman, and John's brother. Church historians suggest that this James was most likely called "the Greater" because he was taller or older than the other James. Zebedee was apparently a fairly prosperous fisherman. Salome, the mother of James and John, later joined other women in following Jesus.

James, John, and another pair of brothers, Peter and Andrew, were closest to Jesus. They were with him at the raising of Jairus' daughter, at the Transfiguration, and during the agony in the Garden of Gethsemane. In Jerusalem, James became the first apostle to die. Herod Agrippa I had him killed with a sword during the Passover of A.D. 44.

James' patronage for pilgrims arises from legends about his journey to Spain. No historical evidence supports the claims for such a trip. But surely James began a great pilgrimage when he threw his nets on the shore to follow Jesus. Canonized: By popular acclaim. Feast: July 25.

Popes
St. Gregory the Great (540–604), Italy

While St. Peter is patron of the papacy as an institution (see p. 31), St. Gregory the Great—the first "Pope Gregory"—is the personal patron of the popes. Though fifteen other Gregorys followed him, it's easy to see why he was so worthy of imitation.

Gregory came from an aristocratic Roman family and was born for leadership. He'd been a magistrate in Rome for many years when suddenly, at age thirty-five, he abandoned it all.

Gregory entered a monastery founded with his own money. If he relished his life as a monk, it didn't last long. The pope sent him to serve in Constantinople. Five years after his return to the monastery, he was elected pope himself.

Gregory's fourteen years as pope were filled with many diplomatic triumphs. He strengthened the Church, sent missionaries to England, wrote about pastoral care and morality, encouraged monasticism, and transformed the liturgy. Without Gregory, Europe would have emerged more slowly from the Dark Ages caused by the barbarian invasions. Canonized: By popular acclaim. Named Father and Doctor of the Church: Eighth century. Feast: September 3.

Preachers
St. John Chrysostom (c. 347–407), Asia Minor

As a boy, John studied rhetoric with one of the best orators of the day. Later, in Antioch, after twelve years as a priest and preacher, John was nicknamed "golden mouth." His sermons focused on Scripture and were profound but practical. They can be appreciated even today.

In 398, John became archbishop of Constantinople. Unfortunately, John's gifts to speak the truth often brought him trouble. He wasn't always tactful in pointing out the sins of the wealthy and powerful.

Despite vigorous objections from the Church in Rome, John was banished twice from his diocese by a coalition of irritated bishops and the emperor. His many letters written in exile are a sad commentary on the state of things in his day. He died of exhaustion on the road as he was being sent still further from home. Canonized: By popular acclaim. Named Doctor of the Church: 451. Named patron saint of preachers: 1909. Memorial: September 13.

Priests
St. Jean-Baptiste Vianney (1786–1869), France

How Jean-Baptiste struggled to become a priest! He grew up in a nation trying to suppress religion. As a seminarian, Jean was drafted by Napoleon's army. Later, his academic progress was so slow that a classmate tutoring him hit Jean in exasperation.

Nevertheless, at age twenty-nine, Jean was ordained. Ars, near Lyons, was Jean's first and only parish assignment. The church was dark and dingy. The parishioners were crude and worldly. But the new curé prayed and fasted for conversions.

Jean founded an orphanage for girls and began daily instructions, and things began to change. His reputation for holiness spread, and he eventually was spending seventeen hours a day hearing confessions. Visitors came from everywhere as area priests complained that Vianney wasn't qualified as a spiritual advisor. Jean agreed and would have preferred a monk's life. But Ars needed him.

Jean died on a sweltering August day in 1869 as his people wept. Canonized: 1925. Named patron of priests: 1929. Feast: August 4.

Retreats
St. Ignatius of Loyola (1491–1556), Spain

While recovering from battle wounds in Pamplona, Ignatius asked for books of romance to pass painful hours. Instead, "Iñigo," as he was called in Spanish, received books about Christ and the saints. In this imposed "retreat," he reconsidered his life and youthful sins.

One night, Ignatius joyfully saw Mary holding Jesus. When the young soldier became well, he hung his weapons by Mary's altar and made a retreat in a cave near Manressa. Here, he began writing *The Spiritual Exercises*, a book that still guides Jesuit retreats today.

Next, Ignatius studied for the priesthood. His early education had been so minimal that he started over with grammar school boys. Nonetheless, he persisted.

Soon his vision of a new religious order gathered others. In Paris, seven men made vows as the "Company of Jesus." In 1540, the pope recognized them as the Society of Jesus. By the time Ignatius died sixteen years later, there were thirty-nine Jesuit houses with missionaries on three continents. Canonized: 1662. Named patron of retreats: 1922. Feast: July 31.

Sacristans
St. Guy of Anderlecht (c. 950–1012), Belgium

Guy came from a poor and pious country family in Brussels. Though uneducated, the boy constantly practiced Christian works of mercy. As a young man, he became sacristan for Our Lady of Laeken Church near Brussels.

For years Guy worked with complete dedication. Then a businessman offered him a partnership and the chance to earn more money for charity. Guy took the offer but soon lost his investment when the ship with their merchandise sank.

Feeling chastised for leaving his sacristan's job, Guy went on several pilgrimages to Rome and the Holy Land. On the way home, several friends in Brussels contracted the plague. Guy cared for them, but they died.

Weakened, Guy returned to Brussels and soon died himself. Stories about miracles at his tomb grew. He was soon seen also as a patron for horses. Brussels cabdrivers annually drove horse-drawn cabs to his grave until the First World War. Canonized: By popular acclaim. Feast: September 12.

Seminarians
St. Charles Borromeo (1538–84), Italy

St. Charles was a cardinal before he became a seminarian! But after all, life was never routine for Charles. He was the second son of a wealthy, prominent count, and his mother was a de Medici.

At age twelve, Charles began seminary studies. In 1559, his uncle, Pope Pius IV, made him a cardinal and the Vatican's Secretary of State! Charles left the seminary and performed magnificently though he had a speech impediment.

When his older brother Federigo died, Charles was pressured to marry and raise Borromeo heirs because he wasn't yet ordained. But he completed seminary studies instead and was ordained. In 1564, he became archbishop of Milan, although Vatican duties kept him in Rome for years.

Charles guided the reforms mandated by the Council of Trent. He established seminaries, "Sunday schools" for the laity, and liturgical reforms. In Milan, he later served as archbishop, though he lived simply. He died suddenly at age forty-six. Canonized: 1610. Feast: November 4.

Tertiaries or Third Order Members
St. Ferdinand III (1198–1252), Spain

Thousands of his Spanish subjects bent their knees to him. But King Ferdinand III of Castille was also routinely on his knees, in prayer. Becoming king of Castille at age eighteen, he was born to lead.

Greatly influenced by his mother, Ferdinand learned to be an honorable king. On his mother's advice, he married Beatrice of Swabia, one of the most virtuous princesses of the day. The couple had a large family.

Ferdinand then gathered the wisest counselors he could find.

He reformed Spanish laws, insisted on justice, and tried not to overburden his people with taxes. He founded the University of Salamanca and built churches and hospitals.

Ferdinand spent twenty-seven years driving the Moors out of most of Spain. He then converted mosques into cathedrals dedicated to the Blessed Virgin, to whom he was devoted. Ferdinand often prayed all night before battle. He was buried in a tertiary's habit, not in a king's robe. Canonized: 1671. Feast: May 30.

Theologians
St. Augustine (354–430), North Africa

Augustine was the oldest of three children. Religious issues were a constant source of difficulty between his Christian mother, Monica, and his pagan father, Patricius. Though raised as a Christian, Augustine didn't practice the faith as a youth. In fact, as a young adult, he lived with a woman and had a son by her.

Though Monica begged him to change, Augustine ignored Christianity and even embraced heresy. Finally, when he heard St. Ambrose preach in Milan, something in that magnificent mind shifted. Suddenly, the young man saw Christ in a new light.

Augustine soon changed his life. After his baptism at age thirty-three, he began to defend Christianity. He was ordained a priest and eventually became a bishop and theologian in Africa. He served the Church there for thirty-four years, opposing heresies and writing spiritual classics such as *The Confessions* and *The City of God*. Canonized: By popular acclaim. Named Doctor of the Church. Feast: August 28.

Vocations
St. Alphonsus Liguori—see *Confessors,* p. 21.

Chapter Two

Patron Saints of Family Life and Home

Adoptive Families
St. Thomas More (1478–1535), England
Young Tom More and his siblings lost their mother while he was still young. They were then lovingly "mothered" by their nurse, Maude. Later, Thomas followed the footsteps of his father John, who was a lawyer and judge. Smart and witty, he studied law and was admitted to the bar in 1501.

Thomas married Jane Holt, and the happy couple quickly had four children. After Jane's death in 1511, the devastated young widower remarried for the sake of his children. Alice Middleton was a cranky but loving stepmother for Thomas' family, which later included an adopted child. He was a busy but loving father to them all.

Thomas became under-sheriff of London in 1510 and attracted the attention of King Henry VIII. Henry named him Lord Chancellor of England in 1529. Because Thomas would not condone the king's divorce and remarriage, Henry imprisoned him and had him beheaded. Canonized: 1935. Feast: June 22.

Childbirth
St. Gerard Majella (1726–55), Italy
Though a sickly child, Gerard became the family's breadwinner and a tailor's apprentice when his father died. Gerard's boss

belittled the boy's religious devotion. But the young man persevered and became a Redemptorist brother.

Brother Gerard was chosen as a spiritual director and visited the sick. Once, however, he was falsely accused of having an affair with a townswoman. When his accuser later confessed her lie, Gerard's superior, St. Alphonsus Liguori, went to him. "Why didn't you deny it?" he asked. Gerard said he had wished to suffer in silence.

Gerard's patronage for pregnant women and women giving birth stems from a story about a handkerchief given to a young woman. During a difficult pregnancy, she held the treasured handkerchief near her womb and was healed. Brother Gerard died of tuberculosis in 1755 at twenty-nine. For generations afterward, the handkerchief associated with the miraculous healing was shared by Italian women about to give birth. Canonized: 1904. Feast: October 16.

Children
St. Nicholas of Myra (fourth century), Lycia, Asia Minor
Nicholas became the bishop of Myra and may have attended the Council of Nicea in 325. Much of his story, however, comes from legends—the kind that children love.

Once, Nicholas met a man who'd lost his fortune. He had no way to support his three daughters and was going to let them become prostitutes. But the bishop intervened one night. He secretly tossed three bags of gold into the man's window.

Gifts lovingly brought in secret at night! That story provides the basis for St. Nicholas Day traditions. Children set out their shoes before his feast. Stockings are hung at Christmas. And "Santa Claus," of course, is a modern but mundane reincarnation of the saint.

Other Nicholas stories report that he saved a sinking ship and brought three murdered boys back to life. The saint's relics are reportedly buried at Bari in southern Italy. Canonized: By popular acclaim. Feast: December 6.

Cooks
St. Martha (first century), Judea

What help can this first-century cook be in modern kitchens? Only heaven knows! What we know here on earth, however, is that Jesus immortalized this committed housekeeper and cook in his own day.

In fact, Jesus told her to find a balance—a balance between domestic and spiritual concerns. "Mary has chosen the better part and it will not be taken from her," the Lord said in reprimand to Martha. She had criticized Mary for listening to his teaching instead of helping prepare the meal (see Lk 10:38-42).

Nevertheless, Jesus never told Martha to avoid cooking and the kitchen. In fact, cooking for a family is a gift of love. A good and healthy meal, shared with others, helps to nourish the body and the soul. Especially in this day when many families don't eat together, the handiwork of family cooks—male and female—is a great blessing for others. St. Martha would have agreed with that. Canonized: By popular acclaim. Feast: July 29.

Couples in Love
St. Valentine (died c. 270), Rome

The legend of this martyred Roman priest dates from the sixth century. Valentine, it is said, was helping Christians during the persecution of Emperor Claudius when he too was arrested. Asked to pay homage to the Roman gods Mercury and Jupiter, this committed priest refused.

In fact, he began to testify for Jesus Christ instead. A prison guard with a blind child then asked for Valentine's prayers, and the girl was healed. The guard's family converted to Christianity, and soon all were led to their deaths.

Valentine, singing God's praises, was led to the Flaminian Way in Rome and beheaded on February 14. Since mid-February was traditionally linked with the pairing of birds in early spring, the beloved Valentine became the lovers' patron. Canonized: By popular acclaim. Feast: February 14.

Difficult or Hurting Marriages
St. Marguerite d'Youville (1701–71), Canada

When her "papa" died, twelve-year-old Marguerite lost her father and financial security. From then on, she helped her grieving mother. At age twenty-one, Marguerite married François d'Youville, but the match wasn't a happy one. François was unfaithful and wasted the money he made selling liquor illegally.

When François died, his widow worked hard to pay debts and raise her two boys, who later became priests. Though poor herself, Marguerite had always reached out to the poor. With other women, she assumed management of the General Hospital of Montreal. The women were soon called the Gray Nuns. They named their hospital "Hôtel Dieu" ("Hotel God") since they accepted so many poor patients for the love of God.

When her beloved hospital burned down in 1766, the aging Mother Marguerite knelt in the ashes and sang the *"Te Deum."* She who had once lost her own father had discovered that her heavenly Father was always with her. Canonized: 1990. Feast: December 23.

Divorced Women and Men
St. Helena (250–330), Bithynia near the Black Sea

Of humble parentage, Helena nonetheless caught the eye of Constantius Chlorus, a Roman general. The two married, and Helena gave birth in 275 to Constantine, the future emperor. In 292, however, Constantius divorced Helena to marry a more politically influential woman.

Was Helena bitter and wounded? We know only that she may have converted to Christianity at this time. Later, when her son Constantine became the Roman emperor, Christianity was finally legalized. Then, "Empress" Helena devoted herself to building Christian churches in the Holy Land.

Helena is associated with the discovery of the cross of Jesus on Calvary. It was a fitting joy for a woman of faith who bore her own personal cross with grace. Helena grew old, rejoicing to see the spread of Christianity. Canonized: By popular acclaim. Feast: August 18.

Dysfunctional or Hurting Families
St. Eugene de Mazenod (1782–1861), France

Day after day, there was bickering in the de Mazenod home. Charles-Antoine de Mazenod and his wife Marie-Rose had little in common. Little Eugene, the eldest child, heard his mother's family belittle his father, a well-educated aristocrat who was suddenly poor. To make matters worse, in 1790 the family had to flee to Italy to escape the French Revolution.

A dozen years later, after his parents had separated, Eugene tried unsuccessfully to reunite and reconcile them. But the couple divorced. Wounded, he struggled with his feelings and his future.

Finally, Eugene was touched by a vision of Christ. He

became a priest and renounced his inheritance. He began to work among the poor in southern France. With a group of priests, he offered parish missions in the region.

In 1826, Eugene founded the Oblates of Mary Immaculate. He helped to rebuild the Church in France and became bishop of Marseilles in 1851. He died of cancer at age seventy-nine. Canonized: 1995. Feast: May 21.

Expectant Mothers
St. Anne (first century B.C.), Galilee
The mother of the Blessed Virgin Mary has long been honored as one of the patrons expectant mothers may call upon. And indeed, she should be, though there is no certain knowledge about Mary's mother. Apocryphal literature, including a book called *The Protoevangelium of James,* suggests that Mary's mother was Anne, the wife of Joachim.

Anne was old and had never born a child. One day, as she prayed for this blessing beneath a laurel tree in her Galilean garden, an angel appeared. "Anne," he said, "your prayer is answered, and you will conceive and bring forth a child. Your seed shall be spoken of in all the world."

In due time, St. Anne did give birth to Mary. Traditional stories tell us that Mary's parents gave her to the service of God when she was three. Devotion to St. Anne developed in the Western Church after the thirteenth century. Canonized: By popular acclaim. Feast (with St. Joachim): July 26.

Fathers
St. Joseph—see *The Church,* p. 21.

Gardeners
St. Phocas the Gardener (dates unknown), Paphlagonia

This legendary hero was innkeeper and gardener in the ancient port city of Sinope in Asia Minor, near the Black Sea. Phocas was a devoted follower of Christ. Though he depended upon his garden for part of his income, he typically shared much of the food he raised with the poor.

One day, soldiers came to his inn boasting about their orders to arrest and execute a Christian named "Phocas." The innkeeper said nothing but treated them with perfect hospitality. During the night, he dug his own grave.

At daybreak, he confessed to the soldiers that he was the man they sought. Phocas did indeed soon lie in the grave he had dug. Perhaps it was near the garden he had worked and loved. This saint is particularly remembered with affection in the Eastern Church. Canonized: By popular acclaim. Feast: September 22.

Grandfathers
St. Joachim (first century B.C.), Galilee

Tradition names Joachim as the husband of St. Anne and the elderly father of Mary. In fact, Scripture named neither the maternal grandfather nor the grandmother of Jesus.

According to the apocryphal *Protoevangelium of James,* Joachim was away from his Galilean home when a messenger told him that he and his wife Anne would have a child in their old age. The messenger, of course, was an angel. Later, when their wonderful daughter was weaned, the holy couple dedicated her to the service of God at the temple.

Joachim's name means "God prepares"—a wonderful name for the grandfather of the Redeemer. Appropriately, Joachim shares his feast—as he shared his life—with St. Anne. Canonized: By popular acclaim. Feast: July 26.

Grandmothers
St. Anne—see *Expectant Mothers,* p. 44.

Grieving Children
St. Marguerite d'Youville—see *Difficult or Hurting Marriages,* p. 42.

Grieving Parents
St. Elizabeth Ann Seton (1774–1821), United States
For a time, Elizabeth Bayley Seton had everything a young woman could want: an adoring and handsome husband, five fine children, and an elegant house on New York's Wall Street. Within a few years, however, she was widowed, poor, and without friends, income, or a home. Desperate for answers, she turned to the Catholic Church and the Eucharist.

Despite strong objections from her family, Elizabeth became a Catholic in 1805. She moved to Maryland to begin the first Catholic school and to found the American branch of the Daughters of Charity of St. Joseph. In Maryland, she was lovingly called "Mother Seton."

In the midst of establishing schools and orphanages for other people's children, Elizabeth lost three of her own: Anna Maria, Becca, and Richard. Only her faith saved her from total collapse and paralyzing grief. Wearied but still full of a motherly love, she continued her work and died of tuberculosis at age forty-seven in 1821. Canonized: 1975. Feast: January 4.

Housekeepers
St. Zita (1218–78), Italy

No one today knows her last name, but memories of Zita's virtues prompted her canonization four hundred years after her death in Tuscany. Zita was twelve years old when she went to work for Pagano di Fatinelli, a wealthy merchant in Lucca. Though simple and uneducated, the girl excelled at her work.

Zita cleaned until things were spotless. She baked and cooked with scrumptious skill. But she was also profoundly prayerful, attended daily Mass, and was devoted to the poor.

Sometimes she gave away food from the Fatinelli pantry. That infuriated her employer. One time, storytellers say, angels were spotted baking the bread Zita had left to tend to a sick visitor. Another time, she emptied the pantry to feed the hungry. When told of this, the angry merchant threw open the pantry door, only to find it miraculously restocked. When Zita died at age sixty, Lucca buried her like a queen. Canonized: 1696. Feast: April 27.

Infertile Couples
St. Rita of Cascia (1381–1457), Italy

The parents of St. Rita had almost given up hope for a child when she was born. Because they were older, they worried about her future. So, at age twelve, Rita was married to a man who soon proved to be an abusive boor.

The couple had two sons. Rita's prayers and love slowly worked a miracle with her husband. But not long after he converted and quit drinking, he was murdered. Rita's boys swore revenge, and she couldn't talk them out of it.

She was heartbroken and prayed that God would not allow her sons to become murderers. Tragically, both boys soon died.

Now widowed and childless, the grieving woman entered an Augustinian convent.

Rita had a great devotion to the passion of Christ. People who asked for her prayers were often blessed with healings or miracles. She received the stigmata and a bleeding head wound, apparently caused by a crown of thorns. Canonized: 1900. Feast: May 22.

In-Law Conflicts
St. Jane Frances de Chantal (1562–1641), France

Agony piled upon agony. That's what the young Baroness de Chantal must have felt. She had been deeply in love with her husband, Christophe, when he was killed in a shooting accident. She felt guilt about her secret hatred for the man who killed her beloved.

Then, deeply depressed, Jane and her four shattered children were forced to live with her seventy-five-year-old father-in-law. Probably bitter about his son's death, the old man threatened to disinherit Jane if she didn't live with him. For seven years, he made Jane's life almost intolerable.

Nevertheless, she endured it all, growing in faith and in a deepening desire to enter religious life. Later, her friendship with St. France de Sales, the bishop of Geneva, showed her the way. When her children were older, Jane founded the Visitation nuns, a largely contemplative order. More than eighty convents had been founded by her death at age sixty-nine. Canonized: 1767. Feast (in the United States): August 18.

Miscarriage and Stillborn Infants
Blessed Dorothy of Montau (1347–94), Prussia

One of nine children, Dorothy knew the joys of a large family. At age nineteen she married Albert, a wealthy sword smith in

Prague. Though she bore nine children, only one child, a daughter, survived to adulthood.

Grieved with so many heartbreaks over children, Albert became bitter. He abused and blamed his wife. Patiently, Dorothy endured his torturing rebukes even as she encouraged him in his work and in his faith.

In 1389, Dorothy left her daughter at home to make a pilgrimage to Rome to pray and lift her spirits. When she became ill, her return was delayed. In the meantime, Albert died at home.

Saddened now by the added loss of her husband, Dorothy became a hermit. She lived in a tiny cell, became known for her holiness and devotion to the Eucharist, and spent her days in prayer. Her daughter, pursuing similar goals, became a Benedictine nun. Canonized: Canonization process begun but never completed. Feast: October 30.

Mothers
St. Monica (331–87), North Africa

"Surely the son of so many tears will not perish," a wise bishop once told Monica, the Christian mother of a son whose life and choices troubled her deeply. Monica and her pagan husband, Patricius, had three children. They could see that their oldest son, Augustine, was exceptionally brilliant.

Tearfully, Monica watched as her talented Augustine slowly abandoned his faith. For seventeen years she wept, prayed, and fasted for this child of hers. She even followed him to Rome and to Milan.

Monica had once dreamed that Augustine would one day change his ways and return to the faith. In 386, her motherly prayers were answered. Augustine was baptized. He would become one of the most brilliant theologians of the Church.

While waiting for a ship back to Africa, fifty-five-year-old Monica died in Ostia, Italy. Devastated, Augustine finally knew the meaning of a mother's love and prayers. Canonized: By popular acclaim. Feast: August 27.

Nursing Homes
St. Catherine of Siena (1347–80), Italy

In the era in which Catherine was born, the Black Plague killed one-fourth of Europe's population. Catherine Benincasa was a twin and the youngest of twenty-five children. In 1374, ten family members contracted the plague. The bright, outgoing Catherine cared for them and then cared for the city's poor and hospitalized.

Ironically, she had once longed for a hermit's life. But Christ said: "The only way you can serve me, Catherine, is in service of your neighbor." A Dominican tertiary, she served tirelessly, visiting many people who were abandoned and forgotten.

On the other hand, Catherine also related to many "celebrities," including Pope Gregory XI. She told the pope to return to Rome and begin reforms. Her conversations with Christ were collected in *The Dialogue*, a classic of mystical literature. Catherine received the stigmata, which remained invisible until her death at thirty-three, when they appeared clearly. Canonized: 1461. Named Doctor of the Church: 1970. Feast: April 29.

Orphans
St. Jerome Emiliani (1481–1537), Italy

Every evening, Fr. Jerome Emiliani returned to his house in Venice with a few more scrawny and famished children. It was all he could do to make enough soup and bread for all. The plague had taken some of their parents. But others were simply abandoned and terrified.

Jerome remembered from his own youth how frightening it was to be alone. He had run away from home at age fifteen after his father died. Then, as a soldier, he had been chained alone in a dungeon. But he escaped after praying to Our Lady, and he carried his chains with him. In a church near Treviso, he hung his chains on the wall in a gesture of thanksgiving and new dedication to God.

Soon, Jerome was welcoming orphans in six Italian cities. To help care for them, he founded the Somascan Fathers. Father Jerome also taught them their catechism because it was not enough to care just for their bodies. At age fifty-six, this friend of orphans succumbed to the plague while caring for the sick. Canonized: 1767. Feast: February 8.

Parents of Large Families
King Louis IX (1215–70), France
Crowned king of France at age eleven, Louis was simultaneously trained to rule and to serve. Dealing with his large family must have often been as challenging as ruling France.

Louis' mother was domineering and jealous of Louis' wife Margaret. Louis and Margaret had eleven children, and for years, they patiently endured the interfering tactics of Queen Blanche. Louis was very fond of his daughter Isabella but was also close to his oldest son and heir, Louis. Tragically, Prince Louis died at age sixteen.

In a sense, the poor and needy of France were also part of the king's family. He treated them with great respect and generosity, inviting them to dinner at his homes. He personally tended to lepers, the blind, and the homeless.

Louis led two failed crusades to the Holy Land. He and his son, Prince John, succumbed to disease in Tunisia. Considered a saint already during his lifetime, Louis was canonized in 1297. Feast: August 25.

Single Men
St. Joseph Moscati (1880–1927), Italy

Nothing was the same for young Joseph Moscati after the death of his older brother Albertwhen Jospeh was a boy. Joseph hardly left Albert's bedside after the latter was thrown from a horse and fatally injured. Later, Joseph prayed to find answers.

Slowly, Jesus in the Eucharist spoke to Joseph's young heart. The boy understood and planned to give his life in a more complete way to Christ and to others. In particular, Joseph wanted to help cure physical pain.

Joseph studied medicine and became a prominent doctor and professor of medicine in Naples. During World War I, he served as a doctor but then returned home. Often, Dr. Moscati prescribed medicines for poor patients and paid for them himself. He began each day with Mass and private prayer. Naples wept when Dr. Moscati died suddenly at age forty-seven after a stroke in his office. Canonized: 1987. Memorial: November 16.

Single Parents
St. Elizabeth Ann Seton—see *Grieving Parents,* p. 46.

Single Women
St. Margaret of Cortona (1247–97), Italy

Margaret, a beautiful and bright girl, expected to marry and raise a family. But her life didn't unfold that way. After her mother's death, her father remarried, and Margaret's stepmother never liked her.

As a rebellious teenager, Margaret met and ran away with a young nobleman. She wanted marriage, but his promises were just that. She lived with him for nine years and had a son.

One day, Margaret followed her lover's whining hound and found his battered, decaying body in the forest. This horrifying discovery was a turning point. She wandered with her child until Franciscans at Cortona welcomed her.

Slowly, Margaret found herself and started a new life. She began to follow Jesus in the spirit of St. Francis. Margaret begged for food, tended to the poor, and founded a hospital. Later, she lived in a church that she had helped repair until her death. Canonized: 1728. Feast: February 22.

Stepparents
St. Leopold (1073–1136), Austria

Unlike modern parents, this busy medieval Austrian ruler probably did little "hands-on" care for his many children and stepchildren. But Leopold was undoubtedly a loving father in the style of his times. At age thirty-three, he married Agnes, the widowed daughter of the Holy Roman Emperor.

Instantly, Leopold became the stepfather for his wife's two boys. They were the emperor's grandsons! Protecting, guiding, and educating these two future rulers as well as his own eleven children was a significant accomplishment.

A model for all of his children, Leopold was more committed to his faith than to his career. He refused the offer of the imperial crown in 1125. Instead, he established three monasteries and strengthened the Church in Austria. Canonized: 1485. Memorial: November 15.

Students
St. Thomas Aquinas—see *Catholic Schools*, p. 19.

Widowers
St. Thomas More—see *Adoptive Families*, p. 39.

Widows
St. Jane Frances de Chantal—see *In-Law Conflicts*, p. 48.

Young Brides
St. Elizabeth of Hungary (1204–31), Hungary
Elizabeth's short life had many tragedies. She was taken at age four to the gossipy German court. Living her childhood in a royal goldfish bowl, she was often stung by criticisms about her piety and charity.

At age fourteen, Princess Elizabeth married Prince Louis, whom she loved deeply. She was soon busy caring for three children and serving the poor. But Elizabeth's critics attacked her charities as excessive.

To avoid their opposition, she once tried to hide bread she was carrying to the poor. When she was discovered, the bread miraculously became roses. In 1221, she learned about St. Francis of Assisi and became a secular Franciscan, building hospitals and schools for her people.

When Louis died in 1227 during the Fifth Crusade, twenty-year-old Elizabeth was shattered. Louis' brother soon usurped control and banished her. When she had found good homes for her children, Elizabeth retreated to a cottage. She prayed and nursed the sick until her own health broke down. She died at age twenty-four. Canonized: 1235. Feast: November 17.

Young Women
St. Teresa of Jesus of the Andes (1900–1920), Chile

A lively, healthy girl, Juanita Fernandez Solar was born in Santiago, the capital of Chile. She was well educated, and she worked hard at school. In fact, Juanita put a lot of energy into everything. She loved to ride horses and visit with her many friends.

But much deeper concerns were also a part of this girl's life. Even when she was very small, Juanita was full of love for God. Her parents saw it and were amazed. Prayer and discussions about faith seemed to bubble out of their daughter.

As a teenager, Juanita sorted things out. She knew that she wanted a life of silence and prayer, not marriage and children. She had no disdain for the choices that most young women make. She simply felt called to a different life. Juanita entered the Carmelite convent at Los Andes in 1919 but died of typhus less than a year later. Canonization: 1993. Memorial: July 13.

Youth
St. Aloysius Gonzaga (1568–91), Italy

Two popes in different centuries named Aloysius as a patron for youth, both young men and young women. Even now, it's easy to see enthusiasm and dedication—youthful qualities—in the short life he lived.

Aloysius was born with plenty of advantages. His family was wealthy and well connected, and they gave him the best education possible. Because he was frequently ill, Aloysius developed a habit of reading the lives of the saints while recuperating.

Reading about the Jesuit missionaries touched him deeply. After many family arguments, he relinquished his rights as the eldest son to his younger brother. Then he entered the Jesuit order at age seventeen and had brilliant academic success.

In 1591 the plague struck Italy hard. Young Aloysius fearlessly helped out. He carried plague victims to the hospital on his back. He soon contracted the contagious disease himself and died at twenty-three. Canonized: 1726. Named patron saint of youth: 1729, 1926. Memorial: June 21.

Chapter Three

Patron Saints of
Work Life and Occupations

Accountants and Bankers
St. Matthew the Apostle (first century), Galilee
Matthew—or Levi, as he is called in the Gospels of Mark and Luke—worked for the despised Roman government. In the region of Capernaum on the Sea of Galilee, Matthew collected taxes from his fellow Jews. Fishermen, tradesmen, farmers, merchants—all of them were assessed a tax that took a heavy share of their meager income.

To say that Matthew was an unpopular man is to state the obvious. Roman taxes were deeply resented. When a Jew collaborated with this Roman injustice, the resentment doubled.

Jesus called Matthew while he was at work, "at the customs post," as Matthew recalls in his Gospel (see Mt 9:9). Without hesitation, Matthew got up, left his responsibilities, and joined Jesus. Tradition suggests that Matthew later died a martyr's death in Ethiopia or Persia. Canonized: By popular acclaim. Feast: September 21.

Actors and Actresses
St. Genesius the Actor (fourth century), Rome
Legends about Genesius are more plentiful than solid facts. Historians say that he was the leading comedian and actor of his day in Rome. Like Emperor Diocletian, Genesius was a pagan.

He headed a theater group that was to perform for Diocletian, who'd launched a vicious persecution against Christians.

Genesius devised a skit to mock Christians and baptism. He had the lead and was to play a dying Christian. But, as the story goes, God upstaged Genesius. In the midst of the play, Genesius paused as though he'd forgotten his lines. He had a vision and was instantly converted to Christ.

"I wish to follow Jesus," he said. But Genesius was no longer acting. Suddenly, there were no snide lines or jokes from him about Christians. Genesius soon told the befuddled emperor about his conversion. Diocletian had the actor tortured and beheaded. Canonized: By popular acclaim. Feast: August 25. (Genesius the actor shares this feast with Genesius of Arles, another fourth-century martyr.)

Advertisers, Communications and Public Relations Personnel
St. Bernardine of Siena (1380–1444), Italy

Like those in advertising and communications today, Bernardine knew how to deliver a message. Yet this Franciscan priest didn't preach full-time until he was thirty-seven. For years, he lived in solitude. Then, in 1417, Bernardine was sent to Milan.

He was so well received there that the people didn't want him to leave. Bernardine traveled up and down Italy. He attacked usury, the practice of lending money at high interest rates. He condemned feuding in this politically charged Renaissance era.

While preaching to vast crowds, Bernardine would dramatically raise a large sign with the letters "IHS," the first three letters of the name "Jesus" in Greek. His messages were clear, persuasive, unforgettable. Though offered the job of bishop three different times, he declined.

In his rare spare moments, Bernardine wrote theological works and set up two theological schools. Weary and in failing health, the "People's Preacher" died on a preaching tour. Canonized: 1450. Feast: May 20.

Archaeologists
St. Damasus I (306–84), Rome

As a Roman, Damasus had a deep love for ancient buildings and cultures. Raised as a devout Christian, he became a priest and an assistant to Pope Liberius. Damasus became pope in 366, in an era of both dangerous and encouraging events for the Church.

The discouraging events: An antipope was elected when Damasus became pope. This imposter was banished but continually harassed the true pope. Heresies lured many new Christians into error.

The encouraging events: Christianity became the official state religion. Seizing the moment, Damasus put his scholarly secretary, St. Jerome, to work translating the Bible. This pontiff also restored the catacombs and built basilicas, shrines, and monuments.

Damasus personally wrote epitaphs for the martyrs as their tombs were restored. He didn't feel worthy to be buried with them. Instead, he was buried with his family in a small church rediscovered in 1904. Canonized: By popular acclaim. Feast: December 11.

Architects
St. Bernward (c. 950–1022), Germany

When both his parents died, little Bernward was entrusted to his uncle, the bishop of Utrecht. In the cathedral school at Heidelberg, Bernward's heart healed slowly. He excelled academically but also in the arts—painting, architectural design, and metal work. The pious youngster often made beautiful chalices and candlesticks.

After he became a priest, Bernward was chaplain for the imperial court. At age forty-three, he became bishop of Hildesheim. Perfectly prepared for his role, he was a wonderful shepherd for his people.

Bernward also continued his patronage of the arts. This bishop often indulged his boyhood interest in precious metal work when he visited workshops. But he also had an eye for the larger work of art. He designed and oversaw the erection of many churches and other buildings. Hungering for a deeper life of prayer and mortification, he retired to a Benedictine abbey shortly before his death. Canonized: 1193. Feast: November 20.

Artists
Blessed Fra Angelico (1387–1455), Italy
Even after six hundred years, it's easy to agree with Fra Angelico's friends who said that his paintings were really prayers. Guido, as Angelico was called, was born in Tuscany. He joined the Dominicans in 1407 with his brother Benedetto. Both were artists, primarily illustrators of manuscripts.

Angelico's gift soon needed a larger format. He began to paint religious subjects. He believed that any painter painting Christ had to be "Christlike." Angelico painted angels with human forms but with the shining light of a sunrise. Eventually, he painted many Scripture scenes and portraits of the saints.

For nine years, Angelico labored hard to decorate the Convent of San Marco. In 1445, the pope had Angelico in Rome painting frescoes in two chapels. Pope Eugenius loved the work so much that he offered to make Angelico archbishop of Florence. Fra Angelico humbly declined but continued working in Rome, where he died and is buried. Beatified: 1982. Memorial: March 18.

Astronauts and Pilots
St. Joseph of Cupertino (1603–63), Italy

Like Jesus, Joseph of Cupertino was born in a stable. After his father died, creditors drove his penniless and pregnant mother from her home. Even as a little boy, Joseph was very different from others his age. At eight, he began to experience ecstatic visions that left him staring into open space. Others couldn't see the profound spiritual truths Joseph saw and heard.

After several failed attempts to join a religious community, Joseph was received by the Franciscans near Cupertino. Despite the fact that he was almost illiterate, he was ordained at age twenty-five. His superiors could see that Joseph had astonishing spiritual gifts—the gifts of knowledge, healing, and levitation. Joseph flew in ecstasy at the least suggestion or sound! He could also hear heavenly music during these "flights."

Joseph led a hidden life in Franciscan houses. His flights disturbed the peace in these houses of prayer. But until his death, nothing could keep this joyful mystic down. Canonized: 1767. Memorial: September 18.

Astronomers
St. Dominic (1170–1221), Spain

While pregnant with him, Dominic de Guzman's mother dreamed she'd given birth to a dog! At his baptism, she visualized a star on his chest. The child soon showed that he was indeed special. A brilliant but kind boy, Dominic once sold his books to buy food for others.

By age twenty-five, Dominic was an Augustinian priest preaching against heresy in southern France. The Albigensian heretics there rejected the body and demanded sexual abstinence, vegetarianism, and rigorous fasts. In 1215, Dominic founded the Order of Preachers (Dominicans). He established friaries all over Europe.

Though a humble, kindly man, Dominic wanted well educated Dominican evangelists. His patronage of astronomers comes from a sign he once saw in the heavens. It prompted his founding of a convent for nuns he'd led from heresy. He died at age fifty-one in a borrowed bed and borrowed Dominican habit. Canonized: 1234. Feast: August 8.

Athletes
St. Sebastian (died 288), Italy

Most of the details about this saint's life will always remain a mystery. Even his birthplace is not known for certain. St. Ambrose wrote that Sebastian was born in Milan. Other sources suggest that he was from Gaul.

Most legends about this early martyr maintain that Sebastian was a Roman officer who hid his Christian identity and practice as long as he could. When the Emperor Diocletian learned of this soldier's secret, he had him shot with arrows. Sebastian survived and was healed through the efforts of St. Irene, the widow of the martyred St. Castulus.

Then, the enraged emperor had his officer beaten to death. Sebastian's physical strength and endurance contributed to his patronage of athletes, who also give their all. He was buried on the Appian Way, and his intercession was linked to many cures from the plague in later centuries. Canonized: By popular acclaim. Feast: January 20.

Authors, Journalists, and Writers
St. Francis de Sales—see *Catholic Press*, p. 18.

Aviators
St. Thérèse of Lisieux—see *Foreign Missions*, p. 26.

Bakers
St. Elizabeth of Hungary—see *Young Brides*, p. 54.

Barbers and Hairdressers
St. Martin de Porres—see *Interracial Justice and Ministry*, p. 28.

Broadcasters (Radio and Television)
St. Gabriel the Archangel
Gabriel, one of the three archangels mentioned by name in Scripture, is often seen as God's messenger. The messages Gabriel carried to earth were most important for salvation history.

It was Gabriel who appeared to Daniel to explain visions relating to the Messiah (see Dn 8:16; 9:21). In the New Testament, Gabriel appeared both to Zechariah and to Mary to tell them about the wonderful children who would be born (see Lk 1:19, 26-27). Gabriel made Zechariah mute until the birth of John the Baptist because the elderly father didn't believe that God's promise could be fulfilled. Traditionally, he's also been identified as the angel who appeared three times to St. Joseph in dreams (see Mt 1:20; 2:13, 19).

Gabriel's role as messenger makes him a fitting patron of other messengers—broadcasters, diplomats, postal workers, and telecommunications personnel. Canonized: By popular acclaim. (with archangels Michael and Raphael) Feast: September 29.

Builders, Construction Workers, and Plumbers
St. Vincent Ferrer (1350–1419), Spain

Vincent was born in Valencia and entered a Dominican seminary at age seventeen. An intellectual prodigy, he taught philosophy at age twenty. He also had great spiritual gifts and was very compassionate.

In 1398, Christ, St. Francis, and St. Dominic appeared to Vincent during a deadly fever. The forty-eight-year-old priest recovered and returned to work with a new fervor. Turning down an offer to become a cardinal, he began preaching about penance and reconciliation all over Europe.

Vast crowds flocked to hear Vincent. A gift of tongues apparently enabled him to be understood in different languages. In Spain, twenty-five thousand Jews became Christians after hearing him preach. He was even asked to mediate political disputes.

Before his workday began, Vincent used to rise at two o'clock in the morning to pray and celebrate Mass. He is a patron for builders, construction workers, and plumbers because he was "on the job" each day and built up the Church. Canonized: 1455. Memorial: April 5.

Business Professionals
St. Homobonus Tucingo (died 1197), Italy

A successful businessman or businesswoman has a product or service to sell, keeps customers happy, and contributes to the well-being of the community. An Italian businessman of medieval Italy did all that and more. Christened prophetically Homobonus ("the good man"), he was the son of a wealthy merchant of Cremona in Lombardy.

Eventually, the son inherited his father's business and prospered. Homobonus did so well that he designated a large portion of his profit to charity. But he also brought his charitable enterprises home. Though his wife disliked the practice, he invited some of his poor friends into his house.

Homobonus was just as faithful to his Church. He attended church each morning and evening, and died suddenly during Mass. So beloved was this businessman to his community that appeals for his canonization received their desired answer in just two years. Canonized: 1199. Feast: November 13.

Cabdrivers
St. Fiacre (c. 595–670), Ireland

St. Fiacre was an Irish priest and monk who became an authority on healing herbs. This expertise, and his reputation for holiness, attracted more visitors than Fiacre wanted. He longed for more solitude. So he emigrated to France in 628 and was welcomed and given land by Bishop (St.) Faro.

The bishop told Fiacre that he could have all the land he could plow in one day. The monk dragged a spade, outlining the acreage he wanted. Trees toppled miraculously. Bushes seemed to be yanked up by invisible hands.

At this new monastery, Fiacre's gift again began to draw many. He often healed with the laying on of hands. Even after his death, Fiacre's monastery served as a shrine. Centuries later in Paris, coaches were first rented out near the Hotel de St. Fiacre. With little images of the saint on the dashboards, the coaches—and later, cabs—were called "fiacres." Canonized: By popular acclaim. Feast: September 1.

Carpenters
St. Joseph—see The *Church*, p. 21.

Composers, Musicians, and Singers
St. Cecilia (second or third century), Rome

Though Cecilia's story can't be historically verified, it presents a worthy Christian parable. Cecilia was a beautiful, young, aristocratic woman whose Roman family arranged her marriage to the pagan Valerian. Privately, Cecilia had already given her life to Christ.

As music played at her wedding, Cecilia sang to God alone. When Valerian learned of Cecilia's vow, she said that an angel accompanied her. When Valerian asked to see the angel, Cecilia challenged him to believe in God and be baptized. Valerian did, and he soon saw Cecilia's angel.

Valerian and his brother Tiburtius became active Christians and were soon martyred. When Cecilia buried them, she too was condemned. A Roman soldier struck her in the neck with a sword, but she died slowly. Her body was reportedly discovered incorrupt in 1599, though it soon deteriorated. Her patronage for musicians dates from the sixteenth century. Canonized: By popular acclaim. Memorial: November 22.

Computer and Internet Users
St. Isidore of Seville (560–636), Spain

In Seville, St. Isidore seemed to have all the knowledge in the world in one place—under his bishop's hat. This brilliant writer, teacher, and churchman wrote a dictionary, an encyclopedia, and a history of the world! At the same time, he oversaw many needed Church reforms.

As archbishop of Seville, Isidore mandated the establishment of a seminary in each diocese and new rules for religious orders. He revised the liturgy and presided over Church councils in Spain. All of this from a man who had been a poor student as a little boy!

Isidore learned early in life to give every situation and problem to God. That simplicity of spirit and his intellectual power made him one of the most brilliant and creative men of his times. His great fund of knowledge and information suggested him as a worthy patron of computer users and the Internet. Canonized: By popular acclaim. Named a Doctor of the Church: 1722. Feast: April 4.

Cooks and Chefs
St. Martha—see *Cooks,* p. 41.

Council Members and Legislators
St. Nicholas von Flue (1417–87), Switzerland
This illiterate saint used his simple gifts well. The son of a farmer, Nicholas was born near Lake Lucerne. He too became a farmer but was also active in local affairs.

In time of need, Nicholas fought in two wars. Once, this very devout farmer-soldier prevented the destruction of a convent. He later married and became the father of ten children.

Nicholas farmed successfully but felt a growing attraction to silence and prayer. With his wife's permission, he retreated to a hermitage at age fifty. All sorts of people visited this hermit noted for his spiritual wisdom.

In 1481, Nicholas helped to settle a dispute that threatened Switzerland with civil war. The rural and urban cantons or states could not agree. But holy Nicholas helped to craft a political compromise that satisfied all. Today, he is still honored by both Catholics and Protestants in Switzerland. Canonized: 1947. Memorial: March 21.

Dairy Workers
St. Brigid (or Bride or Briege)—see *Nuns,* p. 31.

Dancers
St. Vitus (died 303), Sicily
According to legends, Vitus (or Guy) was the son of a Sicilian senator and lived in southern Italy. At age twelve, Vitus became an enthusiastic Christian convert, and he evangelized others as he grew up. Miracles were soon connected with the young believer.

It's said that Vitus healed the Emperor Diocletian's son of an "evil spirit"—possibly epilepsy. Pagans scoffed at Vitus, maintaining that he was a sorcerer. Meanwhile, Diocletian ordered a persistent persecution and elimination of Christians. So Vitus was martyred in the Lucanian province.

Some traditions state that Vitus died with his former nurse Crescentia and her husband Modestus. He later became a patron for those suffering from epilepsy and similar nervous conditions, including "St. Vitus Dance." In sixteenth-century Germany, some people clung to the superstitious belief that dancing before a St. Vitus statue guaranteed a year of good health. Hence his convoluted patronage for dancers. Canonized: By popular acclaim. Memorial: June 15.

Dentists
St. Apollonia (died 249), Egypt
Christian persecution during the reign of Rome's Emperor Decius set new standards for cruelty and inhumanity. During this era, Apollonia was a tortured but unbowed victim. Recovered correspondence from Bishop Dionysius of Alexandria preserved her story.

Apollonia was apparently a deaconess in the Christian community at Alexandria, Egypt. She had high visibility in the strong and stable church community there. When a pagan Roman poet predicted a calamity, the pagan masses were more than ready to blame the coming difficulties on Christians.

As Roman authorities looked aside, gangs began to kidnap and torture innocent Christians with ghastly cruelty. Apollonia was beaten so badly that all her teeth were broken. Then she was told to repeat blasphemies or face death by fire. She broke free and leaped willingly into the raging bonfire, dying a martyr's death. Canonized: By popular acclaim. Feast: February 9.

Diplomats
St. Gabriel the Archangel—see *Broadcasters (Radio and Television)*, p. 63.

Drivers and Transportation Workers
St. Christopher (third century), Canaan
Many legends but few facts are connected to this popular saint. So Christopher's name was removed from the Church calendar in modern times. "Offero," as he is also known, was reportedly born in Canaan, near the Jordan River.

A huge, strong man, Offero was wandering the world when he met a Christian hermit who lived near a dangerous stream. The old man directed travelers to places for safe crossing. The hermit instructed Offero in the faith and then asked him to take over his job.

Instead of directing travelers, Christopher carried them across the stream on his back. One day, Christopher carried a small child whose weight almost drove him underwater. On the other side, the boy said: "Don't be surprised. You have been carrying the weight of the world's sins. I am Jesus Christ, the king you seek." Christopher (or "Christ bearer") was martyred about 251, during the persecution of Decius. Canonized: By popular acclaim. Feast: July 25.

Ecologists
St. Francis of Assisi—see *Catholic Action,* p. 17.

Editors
St. John Bosco (1815–88), Italy
When John was only two years old, his father died, leaving John's mother with no income and three boys. But as John later fondly recalled, "Mama Margaret" gave her sons a good religious education and saw them as her treasure.

To help make ends meet, John did odd jobs. But he was also full of fun. He collected jokes, learned ventriloquism, and mastered juggling and acrobatic stunts. He often led his chuckling audience in prayer after a show.

As a teenager, John caught the eye of a local priest. He helped John enter a seminary, while a nearby village paid his tuition with eggs, butter, and milk. After ordination, Father Bosco went to Turin to aid homeless boys.

To help his boys, he built orphanages, schools, and workshops, including printing and bookbinding shops. To expand ministry to children, John founded the Salesian Order for men and the Daughters of Our Lady, Help of Christians for women. Canonized: 1934. Feast: January 31.

Emergency Medical Technicians (EMTs)
St. Michael the Archangel
In a homily, Pope St. Gregory the Great (A.D. 540–604) once said, "Whenever some act of wondrous powers must be performed, Michael is sent." St. Michael, one of the archangels, brings messages of extreme importance to the world. One of the three archangels referred to in the Bible—along with Gabriel and Raphael—Michael was called the protector of the Chosen People (Israel) in the Book of Daniel.

In the Book of Revelation in the New Testament, Michael throws the devil and all demons out of heaven. Among Muslims, Christians, and Jews, devotion to Michael as a defender against many kinds of evil is common. In the sixth century, Michael reportedly appeared on Mount Gargano in Italy. Canonization: By popular acclaim. Memorials: May 8, Apparition of St. Michael and Protector of Cornwall; September 29, Feast of the Archangels Michael, Raphael, and Gabriel.

Engineers
St. Ferdinand III—see *Tertiaries or Third Order Members*, p. 37.

Farmers
St. Isidore the Farmer (1070–1130), Spain
A son of the soil, Isidore was born near Madrid. Every account of this saint insists that he was extraordinarily pious, charitable, and faithful. Simple, quiet virtues—but these virtues were the seeds of this farmer's holiness.

Day after day and year after year, Isidore tended the fields of Juan de Vergas, his employer. The hired man never had another job. He attended Mass each morning before coming to work.

Isidore and his wife, Maria, also a saint, had one son who died in childhood. Their generosity to the poor, given their meager livelihood, was well known. Fanciful stories of angels plowing Isidore's fields for him multiplied after his death at age sixty.

Isidore's cause for sainthood finally moved beyond the cult of miracle stories and fanciful tales. King Philip III of Spain attributed his recovery from a serious illness to Isidore's intercession. Canonized: 1622. Feast: May 15.

Firefighters
St. Florian (died 304), Rome
Though ancient, stories of Florian appear to be solid and consistent. Florian was a high-ranking Roman officer in Noricum, in present-day Austria. Somehow, he came to believe in Christ.

Since he was serving the empire during the reign of Diocletian, a rabid persecutor of Christianity, Florian knew his days were numbered. When he received orders to execute a group of Christians, he refused and surrendered himself to Aquilinus, the Roman governor of the region. Florian confessed his new faith and was immediately scourged.

His agonies were intensified when he was half-flayed. Then, his poor body was set on fire, and he was thrown into the Enns River with a stone tied around his neck. Thus Florian's death came through both fire and water. Christians of the area retrieved his body. He was buried at Linz, Austria, and still later in Rome. Canonized: By popular acclaim. Feast: May 4.

Fishermen
St. Peter the Apostle—see *Papacy*, p. 31.

Florists
St. Thérèse of Lisieux—see *Foreign Missions*, p. 26.

Forestry and Park Workers
St. John Gualbert (died 1073), Italy
This saint, the son of a noble family of Florence, found God as he was about to kill someone on Good Friday. John's brother had been murdered, and John tracked down the murderer. He was about to kill the man when a vision of Christ crucified stayed his hand and touched his heart. He let the murderer go free and began to pursue God.

John became a Benedictine monk but soon found that life too "easy." He founded another community, and with a group of monks John carefully cut timber and gathered mud near Fiesole in northern Italy. They built their monastery at Vallombrosa.

Abbot John was later known there for his charity, poverty, and gifts of prophecy and healing. His patronage for forestry and park personnel may seem ironic to those who support the leaving of forests untouched. But John used—and didn't abuse—resources God provided. Canonized: 1193. Memorial: July 12.

Funeral Directors
St. Joseph of Arimathea (first century), Judea
As St. Luke says, Joseph was a "virtuous and righteous" man who was also a follower of Jesus (see Lk 23:50-51). Joseph received the body of Jesus from Pilate. Then, as St. Mark's Gospel says, "he took him down, wrapped him in a linen cloth and laid him in a tomb that had been hewn out of rock" (see Mk 15:43-46). Joseph handled a sad task with tenderness and respect.

Legends about Joseph began to circulate in the fourth century. By the thirteenth century, the legends had grown more fanciful and intriguing. It was said that the apostle Philip sent Joseph as a missionary to Britain, and that Joseph established a church at Glastonbury. Other legends intertwined Joseph with the Holy Grail, the cup Christ used for wine at the Last Supper. These legends eventually involved King Arthur and the Knights of the Round Table. Canonized: By popular acclaim. Memorial: March 17.

Gardeners
St. Phocas—see *Gardeners,* p. 45.

Horsemen and Horsewomen
St. Martin of Tours (c. 316-97), France
Martin, the son of a Roman tribune, was born in Hungary. At age fifteen, Martin became a soldier like his father. One cold night at Amiens, France, Martin met a shivering, half-naked beggar. The soldier got off his horse and cut his heavy cloak in two, giving one half to the old man.

In a dream, Martin later saw the old man as Christ. That changed his life. He left the army and was soon baptized by St. Hilary. At first, Martin became a hermit at Ligugé. Others joined him in establishing an early monastery that later became Benedictine.

In 371, the clergy of Tours made Martin their bishop. The people of Tours were delighted. Still treasuring solitude, the bishop was nevertheless always welcoming and loving.

Martin traveled tirelessly, teaching and opposing heresies. He also pleaded for the pardon of heretics condemned to death. Wearied but still active at age eighty, Martin died at Candes.

Canonized: By popular acclaim soon after his death. Feast: November 11.

Hospital Administrators
St. Frances Xavier Cabrini (1850–1917), Italy and the United States

After she nearly died at age twenty from smallpox, Frances Xavier Cabrini stayed away from hospitals. In 1887, she founded the Missionary Sisters of the Sacred Heart of Jesus in Italy. In 1889, she brought her sisters to America.

Pope Leo XIII urged her to go west rather than east to Asian missions. Many Italian immigrants needed help in America. One night, however, Mother Cabrini dreamed that Our Lady was tending people in a crowded hospital. "I'm doing this because you refused to," the Virgin said. Mother Cabrini had previously refused to found Catholic hospitals. Now she obeyed God's will.

This energetic woman founded Columbus Hospital in New York City, as well as hospitals in various other cities, including Chicago, where she died in 1917. In all, she founded fifty institutions. She would often challenge her weary sisters by asking, "Who is doing this—we, or the Lord?" Canonized: 1946, the first U.S. citizen to become a saint. Memorial: November 13.

Hotel Personnel
St. Martin of Tours—see *Horsemen and Horsewomen,* p. 74.

Housekeepers and Maids
St. Zita—see *Housekeepers,* p. 47.

Hunters
St. Hubert (656–727), France

For Hubert, the carefree, oldest son of the Duke of Aquitaine, hunting was a passion. He was popular at the court in Austrasia and met and married the lovely Floribanne.

On Good Friday in 682, Hubert was out hunting since remembering Christ's death meant little to him. As he urged his horse in pursuit of a handsome stag, the stag turned and spoke to him. The overwhelmed Hubert saw that there was a cross between the stag's antlers.

"Unless you turn to God, you will be lost," the stag said. Hubert's life changed overnight. When his young wife died shortly after, he entrusted his baby son to his brother, gave up his inheritance, and became a priest.

Hubert eventually became bishop at Maastricht. He converted many pagans in the Ardennes forest region, pursuing souls for God as he had once hunted prey. Canonized: By popular acclaim. Feast: November 3.

Jewelers and Metal Workers
St. Eligius (588–660), France

The Roman parents of Eligius settled in Gaul (France). His father saw that this son was extremely artistic. So young Eligius was soon apprenticed to the master of the mint at Limoges.

The young man's skills caught the eye of King Chlotar II, who made him mint master at Marseille. There, Eligius, always a strong and faithful Christian, began to give much of his income to ransom slaves, feed the poor, and build churches. He also founded monasteries and convents.

With a group of men, Eligius lived according to Irish monastic rule. At age fifty-two, he and his friend Dado were ordained priests. In 640 he was called by the clergy and faithful of Noyon-Tournai to become bishop. Eligius accepted and proceeded to teach and preach for the next twenty years to convert pagans in his diocese. Some of his sermons still exist. Canonized: By popular acclaim. Memorial: December 1.

Law Enforcement Personnel
St. Michael the Archangel—see *Emergency Medical Technicians*, p. 71.

Lawyers
St. Ivo (or Yves) (1253–1303), France
"A man with his heart set on justice." That's the way the people of Brittany still remember this patron saint of lawyers who received degrees in both civil and canon law. He was born at Kermartin and was the son of a wealthy Breton landowner.

As a young lawyer, Ivo was appointed a diocesan judge for the bishop of Rennes. He was soon highly respected for his honesty and fairness and absolute refusal to take bribes. Ivo always cared for the poor, often taking their cases to court for free. He even resisted unjust taxes levied by the king.

In 1284, at age thirty-one, Ivo was ordained a priest and settled into full-time parish work. He fasted, had a rich prayer life, and lived simply. He was later linked to many wonders, including the feeding of hundreds from a single loaf of good Breton bread. Canonized: 1347. Memorial: May 19.

Librarians
St. Jerome (347–419), Dalmatia
One of the most learned men of the early Church, Jerome was born to a wealthy family and educated in Rome. Though raised

as a Christian, he was not baptized until the age of eighteen. He was deeply touched by the catacombs and stories of the early Christian martyrs.

A brilliant linguist and scholar, Jerome translated and copied many books after entering religious life. Despite his quick temper and difficult personality, he set up several successful monasteries. In 381, Pope Damasus put Jerome to work translating the Bible into Latin for the common people.

When Damasus died, Jerome and his supporters moved to Bethlehem and set up three monasteries. There, he spent his remaining thirty-six years translating the Old Testament and writing. A touching but highly dubious legend says that Jerome died with his head in the manger in which Baby Jesus had slept. Canonized: By popular acclaim. Named Church Father and Doctor of the Church: eighth century. Memorial: September 30.

Linguists
St. Gottschalk (died 1066), Germany

A warrior who had a way with words, Gottschalk was a German prince at a monastery school in Lenzen when his father was murdered by a Christian Saxon. When the boy heard of his father's death, he grew enraged, renounced his faith, and lived for revenge. Gathering supporters, Gottschalk attacked Saxons and killed many.

But his forces were too small. Gottschalk was taken prisoner, and his lands were forfeited. When released, this disheartened prince emigrated to Denmark and began to fight for Denmark.

In the meantime, Gottschalk married and returned to the faith. When the time was right, he returned to his homeland and was restored to power and his lands. Then he used his skills to establish monasteries and churches and to bring priests to his people.

Fluent in many tongues, Gottschalk would often translate the priests' sermons and instructions. When some tribes revolted against the Christian faith, Gottschalk and others were murdered. Canonized: By popular acclaim. Memorial: June 7.

Medical Workers
St. John Regis (1597–1640), France

Even as a boy, John Regis was intense and seldom enjoyed a vacation. This son of wealthy, noble parents longed to please. But God worked with the young man's insecurities, and he began to relax.

John entered the Jesuits. He studied hard but also taught catechism to children near Auvergne in southern France. He was so persuasive that some of the children's parents even returned to the faith. This became the pattern for his ministry.

When John ministered to plague victims in Toulouse, he didn't try just to save lives. He worked tirelessly to change unhealthy social conditions and lifestyles as well. Despite death threats, John found lodging and honest work for prostitutes. Many of them reformed. He also pressed wealthy Catholics to support the poor.

Sensing that his death was near, John prayed for three days, then returned to work and died of pneumonia at forty-three. Canonized: 1737. Memorial: December 31.

Merchants and Sales Personnel
St. Francis of Assisi—see *Catholic Action*, p. 17.

Midwives
St. Margaret of Cortona—see *Single Women*, p. 52.

Mountain Climbers
St. Bernard of Methon (923–1008), Switzerland

There's a good reason why St. Bernard dogs are named after this medieval saint. Like their namesake, the dogs are faithful, selfless, and dedicated to heroic service in the snowy Alps.

Born to a wealthy family in Savoy, Bernard refused a marriage proposed by his father because he wanted to serve the Church. He was an excellent student and was soon ordained a priest. In 966, Bernard became the chief assistant of the bishop of Aosta, Switzerland.

In this isolated region, people were ignorant and trapped in idolatry. Shocked, Bernard got to work. For forty-two years, he preached the faith. He established a monastery and hospice for travelers headed for Rome through the Pennine Alps.

At times, snowdrifts towered forty feet high near Great St. Bernard Pass. Monks and their large, trained dogs would search for those lost in the snow. St. Bernard died in 1008. Canonized: 1681. Feast: May 28.

Naval Officers and Personnel
St. Francis of Paola (1416–1507), Italy

There was an early bond between Francis of Paola and St. Francis of Assisi, who had lived two hundred years earlier. Baby Francis developed a swelling that threatened to blind one eye. His parents interceded with St. Francis, promising that little Francis would spend a year in a Franciscan house.

Francis did just that as a teenager. He was drawn to monastery life and became a hermit. Then others joined him. In 1454, he wrote a new rule for his followers, whom he called the Hermits of St. Francis or the Minims, meaning "least" of all religious.

The hermit's gifts of prophecy and healing were soon widely known. The pope sent Francis to the dying king of France, who had begged to see him. The king's heirs detained Francis, and he died in France at age ninety-one. His frequent travels by water seem to account for Francis' patronage of seamen. Canonized: 1512. Feast: April 2.

Nurses
St. Camillus de Lellis (1550–1614), Italy

Caring for the sick? That never would have appealed to a tall, well-built soldier who'd found his home in the army. Camillus de Lellis was also a compulsive gambler who'd lost everything he had.

But one day, the penniless soldier went to Mass and heard a sermon that turned his life around. He began searching for meaning in his life. In Rome, St. Philip Neri became his confessor, and Camillus began to work at San Giacomo Hospital.

He found it poorly run. Patients were shockingly mistreated. When put in charge, Camillus reformed patient care and studied for the priesthood. He isolated contagious cases, instituted healthy diets, opened windows for fresh air, and obtained hospital chaplains.

After ordination, Camillus founded the Congregation of the Servants of the Sick, an order of priests and brothers to nurse the sick. He saw Christ in his sick patients. Canonized: 1746. Memorial: July 14.

Orators and Public Speakers
St. John Chrysostom—see *Preachers,* p. 34.

Painters
St. Luke the Evangelist (first century), Antioch

This Gospel writer may have been the son of pagan slaves. Luke was a physician, but it wasn't uncommon for families to educate slaves to provide family physicians. About the year 51, Luke joined St. Paul and was with him on many missionary journeys.

Luke had converted to Christianity and wished to serve Jesus. His motivation to write one of the four Gospels must have come from his ministry with Paul. Luke's Gospel and his Acts of the Apostles show great sensitivity to Jesus as healer and gives attention to the Gentiles. Only Luke tells the parable of the Good Samaritan.

Traditional stories say that Luke painted several portraits of Mary, but these can't be substantiated. Rather, it's the portraits Luke created with words in Scripture that inspired many painters and artists. This work justifies his patronage of painters. Luke died in Greece at age eighty-four. Canonized: By popular acclaim. Feast: October 18.

Paratroopers
St. Michael the Archangel—see *Emergency Medical Technicians,* p. 71.

Pharmacists
St. Gemma Galgani (1878–1903), Italy

Gemma was the oldest of eight children whose father was a hardworking but underpaid pharmacist. Friends liked the kind, quiet, and pious girl and saw that she was extremely devout. Gemma's mother died when she was seven, and her father died twelve years later.

Gemma took care of her younger siblings until she contracted spinal meningitis. She almost died but was cured through the intercession of St. Gabriel of Our Lady of Sorrows. In 1899, Gemma received the stigmata. These wounds of Christ appeared each Thursday and Friday for several years.

For many years, Gemma also experienced many ecstasies and mystical experiences. These included visions of her guardian angel and the devil. She tried to join religious communities but was rejected because of poor health. She died at age twenty-five of tuberculosis. Her father's identity as a pharmacist led to her identification as patron for pharmacists. Canonized: 1930. Memorial: April 11.

Philosophers
St. Justin (c. 100–165), Samaria

Philosophy was in Justin's blood. Born to pagan Greek parents in Palestine, he studied one philosophy after another. He truly searched for truth. At age thirty, he thought that Platonism would help him be happy and understand life. But he was honest and knew that he was not yet happy.

One day, near the sea, Justin met an old man who suggested that Christianity—not Platonism—was the answer. For the first time, Justin read Scripture. There, he found the truth, God, and happiness all at once. He was soon baptized and began to travel and teach about Christianity.

With six others, Justin was arrested in Rome in 165. The Roman prefect Rusticus questioned him and ordered him to worship Roman gods. Justin refused, saying, "No right-minded man forsakes truth for falsehood." Justin was tortured and beheaded. Canonized: By popular acclaim. Memorial: June 1.

Physicians and Surgeons
St. Luke the Evangelist—see *Painters,* p. 82.

Poets
St. David (c. 1040-970 B.C.), Israel
David, an Old Testament saint, is listed in the Roman calendar for a very good reason. He was the second king of Israel and an ancestor of Jesus. David was told by God that the Messiah would come from his descendants.

This patron saint of poets undoubtedly composed his first prayerful poems in the hills around Bethlehem. He was a shepherd, caring for his father's sheep. David was the youngest of Jesse's eight sons. He became king around 1010 B.C.

King David established Jerusalem as Israel's capital but left the building of God's temple for his son, Solomon. David's adultery and murder of Bathsheba's husband were repulsive in God's sight. But David repented and won God's favor again.

The beautiful psalms of David have touched the faith and spirits of believers for three thousand years. He died in Jerusalem at age seventy and was buried at Mount Zion. Canonized: By popular acclaim. Memorial: December 29.

Politicians
St. Thomas More—see *Adoptive Families,* p. 39.
St. Thomas was named the patron saint of politicians by Pope John Paul II in October 1999.

Postal Employees
St. Gabriel the Archangel—see *Broadcasters (Radio and Television),* p. 63.

Printers
St. John of God (1495–1550), Portugal

In his early days, John was a man of action, not of books. Born in Portugal, he was a shepherd boy. As he grew up, John was restless and wanted adventure. He became a mercenary soldier and moved to Morocco to sell slaves.

John did many things he later regretted. Settling in Gibraltar in his thirties, the former soldier opened a bookstore and also sold religious icons. One day at Mass, he heard a sermon that hit him hard.

John screamed and began to pound his chest. Bystanders assumed that he'd gone mad! But John of Avila, the preacher, knew better and had the penitent released.

From that day, John devoted his talents to good deeds. He opened a hospital for the poor in Granada. He died of a heart attack after saving a drowning man. Canonized: 1690. Memorial: March 8.

Publishers
St. John the Apostle—see *Friendship,* p. 26.

Radiologists
St. Michael the Archangel—see *Emergency Medical Technicians,* p. 71.

Sailors
St. Brendan the Navigator (486–578), Ireland

Brendan was born near Tralee and was educated by two saints before he became a priest and monk. He founded Clonfert Monastery in Galway about 560. The monastery attracted many men and was a vibrant religious center for a thousand years.

Legends say that Brendan received the rule for his monks

from an angel. Fanciful stories were later pieced onto the bare-bones history of this saint. One legend, "Brendan's Voyage," tells of Brendan and his monks boldly sailing the high seas to evangelize.

The voyagers reportedly came to the Canary Islands off the coast of Africa. At one point, they landed on a small island to light an Easter fire and discovered that their "island" was the back of a whale. Brendan's crew also reportedly discovered America during a seven-year voyage. In fact, however, Brendan probably sailed only to Scotland, western Britain, and islands off the west coast of Ireland. Canonized: By popular acclaim. Memorial: May 16.

Scholars
St. Bede the Venerable (673–735), England

Bede was born in Northumbria, England, when Christianity had finally been firmly planted there. At age seven, he went to school at Sts. Peter and Paul Abbey near Wearmouth. There, he grew up to become a scholar and priest. In fact, he never really left this abbey.

Bede's most important scholarly contribution was as a historian. *The History of the English Church and People* was his invaluable account not only of Church history but also of secular history in early England. He was the most learned man of his times, and his writings on grammar, music, and culture served as resources for historians for centuries.

Bede first suggested dating the historical era from the birth of Christ. He is called the father of English history. He died amidst his brother monks, while dictating—almost with his last breath—a translation of John's Gospel. Canonized: 1931. Named Doctor of the Church: 1899. Memorial: May 25.

Scientists
St. Albert the Great (1206–80), Germany

On long walks across Europe, Albert made notations and collected specimens and drawings of insects, plants, and trees. This natural scientist and Dominican friar was trained at the University of Padua. He had a scientist's natural curiosity and respect for methodical thinking.

Albert's interests were broad. He studied the heavens as well as the earth, making valuable observations for astronomers, biologists, botanists, and geologists. But his family wouldn't have approved of his hiking. This oldest son of a noble German military family had joined the new Dominicans against his family's wishes.

In Paris and Cologne, Albert taught theology to Thomas Aquinas. He also studied Greek and Arabic science and showed their basic compatibility with Christian thought. He served as Dominican director of studies and bishop of Regensburg. Albert was canonized and named Doctor of the Church in 1931. He was also named patron of students of the natural sciences. Memorial: November 15.

Secretaries and Clerks
St. Genesius of Arles (died 305), France

This patron saint of secretaries lived by his skills: writing and taking shorthand. Born in Arles in southern France, he was well respected and a true asset to his employer, the magistrate of Arles. But Genesius was secretly a catechumen on his way to becoming a Christian.

One day, the magistrate Maximianus began to dictate a decree that was to be copied and distributed en masse. Genesius was shocked to realize that the magistrate was decreeing the persecution of Christians. With courage, the secretary threw down his writing instruments and denounced the decree. In a moment, the secretary was imprisoned and soon afterward was martyred. Canonized: By popular acclaim. Feast: August 25. (Genesius of Arles shares this feast with Genesius of Rome, another fourth-century martyr.)

Skaters
St. Lidwina of Schiedham (1380–1433), Holland

At the age of sixteen, pretty Lidwina was coaxed into a skating outing after an illness. A friend knocked her down so hard that Lidwina's right rib was broken. The only daughter of Peter and Petronella was carried home in excruciating pain.

The doctors didn't know how to set it, and the wound festered horribly. An agonizing torture began for the girl who'd already turned away suitors to devote her life to God and Our Lady of Shiedam. She endured many years of pain.

But Lidwina's suffering took on a mystical power. She developed the stigmata and great spiritual gifts. Many people, including Thomas à Kempis, visited her. For years, Lidwina's only food was the Eucharist. Miracles occurred near her bed, where she took her last painful breaths at age fifty-three.

After Lidwina died, her body was miraculously restored. She looked again like that pretty teenager who'd gone to skate on the frozen canal. Canonized: 1890. Feast: April 14 (June 14 in Holland).

Skiers
St. Bernard of Methon—see *Mountain Climbers,* p. 80.

Social Workers
St. Louise de Marillac (1591–1660), France

In seventeenth-century Paris, few people gave the hordes of orphans a second look—or even a coin. Criminals often controlled the children and even mutilated them to enhance their begging "appeal."

Louise de Marillac Le Gras, a widowed and well-educated social activist, longed to help the suffering and neglected poor. She had married and had a son, but she sensed that she'd bypassed her true vocation to religious life. After her husband died, Mademoiselle Le Gras began to help the poor.

With "Monsieur Vincent" (St. Vincent de Paul), she organized the Daughters of Charity, a new kind of women's religious community. The daughters visited the sick and suffering and weren't confined to a convent. Highly successful and soon accepted, they were known as the "Gray Sisters." Napoleon once dismissed the impact of philanthropists with the remark: "Give us a Gray Sister anytime!" At the death of Louise, there were over forty houses of the Daughters of Charity. Canonized: 1934. Memorial: March 15.

Soldiers
St. Joan of Arc (1412–31), France

"I am a poor girl; I do not know how to ride or fight," this teenager repeatedly told God. Though she was an illiterate peasant girl, heaven had been calling her to defend France as a soldier. So she obeyed the call, serving with a skill and a selflessness that any soldier could admire.

Joan's "voices" and visions of Sts. Michael, Catherine of Siena, and Margaret had begun at age thirteen. Despite her early reluctance, the pious and charitable "Maid of Orleans" was committed to God's will. At age sixteen, she understood that she was to restore the rightful heir to the French throne.

For fifteen months, Joan courageously led men into battle. But she was finally wounded, captured by soldiers of Burgundy, and sold to England. Joan was tried on trumped-up charges as a heretic. Cruelly treated and abandoned by Charles VII, the nineteen-year-old never failed in courage. She was burned at the stake in Rouen and died repeating the name "Jesus." Canonized: 1920. Memorial: May 30.

Students
St. Thomas Aquinas—see *Catholic Schools,* p. 19.

Swimmers
St. Adjutor (died 1131), France
There are very few established facts connected with the life of this saint. But what is known about him provides the story line for a very exciting tale. Adjutor was a Norman lord and knight who fought in the Crusades. He traveled by boat to the Holy Land and was captured there by the Muslims.

Adjutor's captors tried to force him to abandon or deny his Christian faith, but he refused. In fact, he escaped, apparently swimming to secure his freedom. Later, when he returned to France, Adjutor saw his life differently. He became a Benedictine monk and lived a life of silence and prayer at Tiron Abbey. Canonized: By popular acclaim. Feast: April 30.

Teachers
St. Jean Baptist de la Salle (1651-1719), France

At age twenty-one, this oldest son of a wealthy Catholic couple from Reims became mother and father for his siblings. Jean had to leave the seminary in Paris to go home when his parents died. Perhaps the task of seeing to his siblings' schooling sparked his later interest in education.

When Jean returned to his own studies and became a priest, he devoted himself to educating boys. He founded the Brothers of the Christian Schools (the Christian Brothers) and gave away his family fortune.

Jean was an innovator. Seeing how teachers struggled, he founded teacher training schools. He instituted the practice of teaching subjects in the native language rather than in Latin. He divided students by grade level rather than having all ages study together, as was the common practice of that time.

This selfless educator also organized high schools and trade schools. Other educators, jealous of his success, often harassed him and denounced his schools, which flourished all over Europe. Jean has been called the father of modern education. Canonized: 1900. Memorial: April 7.

Telecommunications Workers
St. Gabriel the Archangel—see *Broadcasters (Radio and Television)*, p. 63.

Television Writers and Television
St. Clare (1194–1253), Italy

At age eighteen, Clare heard St. Francis preaching in Assisi's streets. Though she had suitors, this wealthy girl wanted to follow Francis. One night, she and her cousin Pacifica ran from her mother's palace to take refuge in a convent in Bastia.

With the help of Francis, Clare founded a new community of sisters who were totally dependent on alms. Clare called this the "privilege of poverty." This "privilege" was often attacked as unwise. But she persisted and mothered her community for forty years.

At night, Clare frequently made sure her nuns were covered up and warm. Her sister Agnes and her widowed mother later joined her. Once she repulsed an attack on her convent by holding up the Blessed Sacrament.

Clare left her house just once—to visit Francis. Visions of a Mass on the wall of her cell when she was ill have made her the patron of television writers and television. Canonized: 1255. Memorial: August 11.

Veterinarians
St. Blaíse (died 316), Armenia

Blase was born in Armenia and became a bishop and martyr there. The son of wealthy parents, he was well educated and served as a physician before becoming a bishop. But he also lived a hermit's life for a while, retreating to a cave during an era of Christian persecution.

Many legends circulated about Blaíse after the ninth century. They told of how sick or wounded animals visited him for help but never disturbed his prayers. When he was found in his cave, pagan soldiers arrested and imprisoned him. It was in prison that he reportedly cured a child choking on a fish bone. For that reason, on his feast day throats are blessed and his intercession is asked to protect the blessed from diseases of the throat.

Blaíse was tortured and then killed by beheading. Because of his reputation as a healer, he was later connected with many altars and churches throughout Europe. Canonized: By popular acclaim. Memorial: February 3.

Workers
St. Joseph—see *The Church,* p. 21.

Chapter Four

Patron Saints of Those With Illnesses or Special Needs

AIDS Patients and Ministers
St. Aloysius Gonzaga—see *Youth*, p. 55.

Alcoholism
St. John of God—see *Printers*, p. 85.

Animals
St. Francis of Assisi—see *Catholic Action*, p. 17.

Arthritis and Rheumatism
St. James the Greater—see *Pilgrims and Pilgrimages*, p. 33.

Battle Danger
St. Michael the Archangel—see *Emergency Medical Technicians*, p. 71.

Bleeding
St. Januarius (died c. 305), Italy
Every year in Naples, a small glass vial of this saint's blood begins to change from a dried, dark powder to a red liquid. The blood of Januarius, an early Christian martyr, was shed about 305 when he was beheaded. Like so many others, Januarius lost his life during the persecution of Diocletian.

Though details about him are scanty, it commonly is said that Januarius was a bishop trying to console and comfort his beleaguered flock. As he visited several in prison, he too was arrested and condemned for his faith. The liquefaction of his blood has been noted and scientifically studied for more than six hundred years. It occurs twenty-eight times a year, including on the saint's feast. Canonized: By popular acclaim. Feast: September 19.

Blindness and Eye Diseases
St. Odilia (died 720), Alsace

Odilia was the daughter of a wealthy nobleman, Adalric, and his wife, Bereswinda. When Adalric discovered that his newborn daughter was blind, he quietly ordered his servants to murder her. She would be unmarriageable and a detriment to a noble family.

Odilia's agonized mother intervened, and the baby was given to a peasant woman and raised till about age twelve. Then the girl was baptized by the bishop. As her eyes were touched with the holy oil, she shouted with surprise and joy. She could see!

Odilia's father was moved and was soon reconciled with her. Rejecting a marriage her father planned for her, Odilia became a nun and founded several convents, including one in her father's castle. She became an abbess and died at Niedermunster in 720. Canonized: By popular acclaim. Feast: December 13.

Bowel or Intestinal Disorders
St. Bonaventure (1221–74), Italy

As a youngster, Bonaventure was healed of a childhood disease when St. Francis of Assisi added his prayers to those of his parents. At age twenty-two, the brilliant young man joined the Franciscans and went to study at the University of Paris. There he met and befriended another intellectual giant—Thomas Aquinas.

At age thirty-six, Bonaventure became Franciscan minister general, and he led his community for sixteen years. He wrote constitutions for the order, strengthened academic preparation for priests, and served as a popular preacher and prolific writer. Nevertheless, this "Second Founder" of the Friars Minor was deeply humble.

When the pope's legates arrived with the cardinal's hat, Bonaventure was washing dishes. He told them to hang it on a tree since his hands were wet and greasy. Bonaventure helped prepare for the Ecumenical Council of Lyons, called to unify the Greek and Latin Churches, but he died during the council. Canonized: 1482. Named Doctor of the Church: 1585. Feast: July 15.

Breast Disease
St. Agatha (died 250), Sicily

According to ancient legends, Agatha was beautiful, wealthy, and a member of a distinguished Sicilian family. But she was also consecrated to God. When the Christian persecution ordered by Emperor Decius began, the scene was set for her heroic and timeless sacrifice.

In Sicily, Senator Quintianus was love-struck and wanted Agatha for his own. When she rebuffed his overtures, he exposed her Christian identity, and she was imprisoned. When Agatha still refused to surrender to Quintianus, she was cruelly tortured.

Quintianus ordered her breasts crushed and cut off. St. Peter appeared to console and heal the young woman, but the cruelties continued. Agatha was thrown onto a bed of red-hot coals and burned alive. When she was near death, an earthquake struck, killing a friend of the magistrate overseeing her execution. The saint breathed her last, thanking God for mercifully calling her home. Canonized: By popular acclaim. Feast: February 5.

Broken Bones
St. Stanislaus Kostka (1550–68), Poland

Maybe Stanislaus never personally suffered from a broken bone. But there must have been hundreds of bruises and sore muscles on his young body. For two years, he was routinely beaten, kicked, and verbally abused in Vienna. It was the boy's own older brother Paul who cruelly persecuted and abused him at the Jesuit College they both attended.

Paul could not accept the strong faith and devotion Stanislaus had. It enraged Paul to see Stanislaus acting "weak" and undignified. But Stanislaus refused to fight back or to write to their father.

Soon after he was healed of a near-fatal illness, Stanislaus determined to join the Jesuits. He walked 350 miles to join them in Rome. He died one year later, at age eighteen, on the Feast of the Assumption. His beautiful life was short but full. Canonized: 1726. Feast: November 13.

Cancer
St. Peregrine (1260–1345), Italy

Like St. Paul, Peregrine spent his youth fighting with Christ's Church. The son of a wealthy couple in Forli, Peregrine enjoyed disparaging the Church. Once, the pope sent St. Philip Benizi as a peacemaker during an uprising, and Peregrine hit Philip in the face. When Philip submissively turned the other check to his attacker, Peregrine was stricken with guilt. Not long after that, he converted to the Catholic faith and joined the Servite Order.

For almost thirty years, Peregrine disciplined his mind and body vigorously. He never willingly sat down. He maintained silence and solitude.

As a priest in Forli, Peregrine was known as a wonderful preacher and confessor. When he developed cancer of the foot, an amputation was scheduled. Knowing how this would limit his priestly service, the priest prayed all night before the surgery. In the morning, he was cured. People flocked to see him even more after that. Peregrine lived until age eighty-five. Canonized: 1726. Feast: May 1.

Child Abuse
Sts. Alodia and Nunilo (died 851), Spain

Some sad stories are unfortunately timeless. The themes repeat themselves in too many places. Sts. Alodia and Nunilo were sisters born in Spain. Their mother was a devout Christian while their father was Muslim. When their father died, their mother remarried.

Her new husband was also a Muslim, a person of high rank in Castile. But this man was also a mean-tempered and violent character who had no love at all for his new stepdaughters. In fact, he ridiculed and verbally abused the girls until they decided to escape by living with their aunt.

Devoutly dedicated to Christ and their vows of virginity, Alodia and Nunilo were living the Christian life they longed for when they were arrested. Their stepfather turned them in as Christians to Muslim authorities. The young women bravely rejected opportunities to deny their faith. They were beheaded on the same day in prison in their own hometown. Canonized: By popular acclaim. Feast: October 22.

Deafness and Hearing Disorders
St. Frances de Sales—see *Catholic Press,* p. 18.

Death Row Inmates
St. Dismas (died c. 30), Palestine
With another thief, St. Dismas was executed alongside Jesus Christ on Calvary just outside the walls of Jerusalem. Christian history knows almost nothing about this man who is called "the Good Thief." But his last words were immortalized in the Gospel of Luke: "Jesus, remember me when you come into your kingdom," Dismas told the dying Jesus (see Lk 23:39-43).

An old Arabic legend also involves Dismas. It is said that when the Holy Family was fleeing into Egypt, they were threatened by bandits. One of the thieves was touched when looking at the faces of the couple and their beautiful baby. He told the others to let this family go. That bandit, the legend says, was the young Dismas. Canonized: By popular acclaim. Feast: March 25.

Desperate Situations or Needs
St. Jude Thaddeus (first century), Galilee
Christian history knows very little about this apostle. Jude may have been the brother of James the Lesser and a relative of Christ through Joseph's side of the family. Jude was said to be the son of Cleophas and Mary. He may have also looked a lot like his cousin Jesus.

In general, Jude seems to have been a man in the shadows during the years he followed Jesus. At the Last Supper, however, he asked Jesus why the Lord was not revealing himself to the whole world. Later, after Christ's resurrection and ascension, Jude became a missionary with Simon in Mesopotamia, Syria, and Persia.

The two were reportedly martyred in Persia. Jude was beaten to death with clubs. He may have been the author of the Epistle of Jude, which urges Christians to persevere despite their circumstances. Hence his ancient and widespread patronage in desperate situations or needs. Canonized: By popular acclaim. Feast (with St. Simon): October 28.

Drought
St. Heribert (c. 970–1021), Germany
Something unsettled Heribert, the wealthy and well-educated son of a German duke. So he spent some time at a monastery, thinking about his life and future. Apparently God spoke to him during that period of silence. He became a priest and then served King Otto III as a chancellor.

At the age of twenty-nine, Heribert was elected archbishop of Cologne and then served as an advisor for the new king, Henry II. Despite his political role, he was, more than anything else, a man of deep prayer and faith. Many miracles were linked with his prayerful intercession, and he was seen as a saint during his lifetime. Once, his prayers even seemed to end a damaging and deadly drought. Heribert founded and endowed a Benedictine monastery and church where he was buried. Canonized: Between 1073 and 1075. Feast: March 16.

Drowning Danger
St. Adjutor—*see Swimmers,* p. 90.

Drug Addiction
St. Maximilian Kolbe (1894–1941), Poland
Born in central Poland, Raymond was the second son of poor weavers who worked at home. At a very young age, he had a

vision of Mary. When she offered him the crown of celibacy or the crown of martyrdom, he chose both.

Raymond joined the Franciscans, taking the name Maximilian, and became a priest. Soon he had founded the "Knights of the Immaculata." This new apostolate produced a monthly magazine, radio programs, and a daily Catholic newspaper, which strengthened the faith of many on the eve of World War II.

When the Nazis occupied Poland, Kolbe knew his days were numbered. He defended the Jews, religious freedom, and Poland's right to independence. Cruelly abused after his arrest in February 1941, he later offered his life at Auschwitz in exchange for that of a married man with children. Although Maximilian was never addicted to drugs, he was executed with a lethal injection of carbolic acid at Auschwitz. He died on the eve of the Feast of the Assumption. Canonized: 1982. Feast: August 14.

The Dying
St. Joseph—see *The Church*, p. 21.

Earaches and Ear Ailments
St. Polycarp (c. 69–c. 155), Smyrna, Asia Minor
Polycarp personally knew "John and others who had seen the Lord." He was a disciple of John and a friend of St. Ignatius of Antioch. He became the bishop of Smyrna (modern Izmir, Turkey) and was a rock of faith for the churches of Asia.

Polycarp opposed heresies with great enthusiasm and once said that he would rather be deaf than "listen to arguments for heretical doctrines." This strong statement later linked him to patronage for those with troubling earaches and ear ailments.

At an advanced age, Polycarp was arrested and told to deny

Christ. "I have served him for eighty-six years.... How can I blaspheme my King and Savior?" he answered. When he was thrown into a fire, the flames arced up over him as his skin turned a golden color. A guard then killed him with a spear. The account of his death was the first authentic narrative of a Christian martyrdom. Canonized: By popular acclaim. Feast: February 23.

Emigrants
St. Frances Xavier Cabrini—see *Hospital Administrators*, p. 75.

Epilepsy
St. Vitus—see *Dancers*, p. 68.

Falsely Accused Persons
St. Philip Howard (1557–95), England
One English queen attended this saint's Catholic baptism while another, Protestant Queen Elizabeth I, sent him to prison. Philip Howard's mother was Catholic, but his Protestant father, William, was the wealthy fourth Duke of Norfolk, who was unjustly beheaded for treason. Some years later, Philip was caught up in Elizabeth's glamorous court and adulterous liaisons.

In 1584, however, he came to his senses. He reformed his life, was reconciled with his wife, Anne, and returned to his Catholic roots with her. But Philip was falsely accused of treason, and his newfound faith had been declared illegal in England. Their second child, Philip's son and heir, was born after his arrest.

For ten years, Philip prayed and read Scripture. He carved a cross into his prison wall. The false charges were eventually dropped. But because he wouldn't deny his Catholicism, Philip wasn't freed or allowed to see his family. Gaunt and ill, he died at age thirty-eight in prison. Many years later, Philip's grandson William also died for the faith, becoming the last martyr of the English Reformation. Canonized: 1970. Feast: October 19.

Fire Danger
St. Florian—see *Firefighters*, p. 72.

Floods
St. John Nepomuk (1345–93), Bohemia
The tragic account of John's cruel death in the Moldau River seems to be the reason for his patronage against floods. But in Bohemia, where he is also patron saint, he would have been welcomed as a protector against any danger.

John was the son of a burgher of Pomuk and studied theology and law at the University of Prague. His legal education prepared him for special roles as a priest. In 1393, the archbishop of Prague made John vicar general.

In the same year, however, King Wenceslaus IV decided to name his own bishop and take an abbey for the new bishop's cathedral. Wenceslaus arrested four churchmen when the Church objected. Only John wouldn't give in and was tortured for two weeks. Finally, on the evening of March 20, the furious king had John chained and thrown from a bridge into the Moldau. Bohemians say that seven stars hovered over the river where their saint died. Canonized: 1729. Feast: May 16.

Gambling (Against Gambling Addiction)
St. Camillus de Lellis—see *Nurses*, p. 81.

The Handicapped
St. Germaine Cousin (1579–1601), France

When Germaine was born with a withered right hand, her father Laurent rejected her. Germaine's mother may have cherished her, but she soon died. Laurent's second wife treated the child with shocking cruelty, forcing her to sleep in the stable or in a cupboard under the stairs. Germaine was beaten, fed scraps, and sent to tend sheep at age nine.

Like the shepherd David, Germaine found God under the open sky. She used a homemade string rosary and used to plant her staff in the ground each morning before she ran off to Mass. The sheep never strayed far from the staff in her absence.

When the girl's stepmother accused her of stealing bread one winter day, wildflowers dropped out of the girl's apron instead. When her father finally invited her to rejoin the household, Germaine declined the offer. One morning in 1601, Laurent found her dead in her cot in the cupboard beneath the stairs. Canonized: 1867. Feast: June 15.

Headache Sufferers
St. Teresa of Avila (1515–82), Spain

As youngsters, little Teresa Cepeda and her brother tried to run away to become martyrs in Africa. Teresa loved God, but she loved parties too. After some teenage affairs of the heart, she became a Carmelite nun near her home in Avila.

For years, Teresa had an easy life but poor health. She suffered stomach difficulties and migraine headaches and was paralyzed for three years. At age thirty-eight she saw the crucified Christ. Then everything changed for Sr. Teresa of Jesus. She turned to God, and Jesus told her to reform the Carmelites.

Against much resistance, Teresa founded new Carmelite

houses devoted to silence and prayer. Before her death in 1582 at age sixty-seven, Teresa founded seventeen convents for women and one house for men. Her works of mystical theology, *The Way of Perfection* and *The Interior Castle,* are spiritual classics. Canonized: 1622. Named first woman Doctor of the Church: 1970. Feast: October 15.

Heart Disease and Ailments
St. John of God—see *Printers,* p. 85.

The Homeless
St. Benedict Joseph Labre (1748–83), France
The oldest of fifteen children born to a shopkeeper of Boulogne, Benedict studied for the priesthood as a boy. Later, he was drawn to solitude, though several monasteries rejected him because of his fragile health. So Benedict became a wandering pilgrim to Christian holy places.

All over Europe he was seen—tattered cloak, a rosary round his neck, a copy of the New Testament in his hand. To eat, Benedict foraged or accepted food. As a sacrifice, he never bathed. He smiled at everyone but said almost nothing.

During his last nine years, Benedict visited Roman churches by day and slept in the Coliseum at night. Romans called him the "Saint of the Forty Hours" or Eucharistic devotion, and often saw him praying before the Blessed Sacrament. He died at age thirty-five in a butcher's back room. A reported 136 miracles connected with him occurred shortly after his death. Canonized: 1883. Feast: April 16.

Lost Items
St. Anthony of Padua (1195–1231), Portugal

Ferdinand de Bulhoens' prominent Lisbon parents doted on him but were happy when he became an Augustinian priest. He later joined the Franciscans when he saw the bodies of martyred friars brought home from Africa.

"Friar Anthony," as he was called, longed for the same fate. But St. Francis of Assisi had other plans for the young scholar. Anthony was sent to preach and teach in Italy. Crowds followed the man they called "wonder worker" and the "hammer of the heretics."

Anthony loved the poor and often preached against usury and greed. Once, a school of fish reportedly gathered near shore to hear him. Another time, the hungry mule of an atheist ignored hay and adored the Eucharist the friar held.

Anthony's help for finding lost things stems from an experience in his own life. A disgruntled novice once stole his treasured book of psalms. Anthony prayed, and the thief returned to religious life with the book. Canonized: 1232. Named Doctor of the Church: 1946. Feast: June 13.

Mental Illness
St. Osmund (died 1099), France

A well-educated Norman count, Osmund probably had no idea that he'd one day be the English chancellor and bishop of an English diocese. The tides of war and political fortunes swept him along to this unexpected destination. In 1066, Osmund's uncle, William the Conquerer, crossed the English Channel, won the Battle of Hastings, and claimed the English crown.

As a priest, Osmund wished to serve his new people well, though many resented all Normans. He built a cathedral at

Salisbury, became an excellent administrator, and remained a man of humble tastes. He enjoyed copying and binding books as a leisure-time activity. Though the process of Osmund's canonization took more than two centuries, many claimed healings at his grave, especially the mentally ill and insane. Canonized: 1456. Feast: December 4.

Poison Protection
St. Benedict of Nursia—see *Monks,* p. 29.

Political Prisoners
St. Maximilian Kolbe—see *Drug Addiction,* p. 102.

Poverty
St. Anthony of Padua—see *Lost Items,* p. 107.

Prisoners
St. Joseph Cafasso (1811–60), Italy
A small man with a big heart. That's how most people saw Fr. Joseph Cafasso. Born to a wealthy family near Turin, Joseph had a privileged background and education. But that didn't eliminate pain from his life. He was born with a deformed spine and was crippled and undersized throughout his life.

Joseph felt God's call and became a priest and theologian. His boyhood pal John Bosco later followed him to the seminary, where Joseph taught theology. But Cafasso's interests went far beyond the seminary.

The little priest served men in prison, where living conditions were filthy and inhumane. He also ministered to sixty prisoners awaiting execution. He heard their confessions, reminded them of God's mercy, and stayed with them until they died on the gallows. Death soon claimed the prison chaplain too. John Bosco preached the homily at Cafasso's funeral Mass. Canonized: 1947. Feast: June 22.

Rape and Sexual Exploitation
St. Maria Goretti (1890–1902), Italy

Maria's twelve years were filled with many family difficulties. In 1899, her father, Luigi Goretti, died of malaria, leaving his widow Assunta with six children. The Gorettis had always been poor. But now, Maria's mother took Luigi's place in the fields so that her family wouldn't starve. At age nine, Maria became the little mother and did the shopping, cooking, mending, and cleaning without complaint.

On July 5, 1902, Alessandro, the nineteen-year-old whose family shared a house with the Gorettis, tried to rape twelve-year-old Maria. She fought him off and begged him to stop. Enraged, he stabbed Maria fourteen times.

Maria died the next day after forgiving her attacker. Years later, in prison, Alessandro was converted following a vision of Maria and attended her canonization with her family. It was the first time that the mother of a saint ever attended her child's canonization. Canonized: 1950. Feast: July 6.

Refugees
St. Frances Xavier Cabrini—see *Hospital Administrators,* p. 75.

Runaways and Missing Persons
Sts. Alodia and Nunilo—see *Child Abuse,* p. 99.

The Sick
St. Camillus de Lellis—see *Nurses*, p. 81.

Snakes (Protection From)
St. Patrick—see *Bishops*, p. 15.

Storm Protection
St. Scholastica (480–543), Italy
The twin sister of St. Benedict of Nursia, Scholastica was as devoted to God as was her brother. She became a nun as a young girl and lived near Monte Cassino, where Benedict's monastery was established. The two were close emotionally and met each year to visit and pray together.

Scholastica's patronage for storm protection comes from an event recorded in Pope St. Gregory's "Dialogues." In 543, secretly sensing that she would die soon, she tried to prolong her brother's visit. But he refused and began to leave.

Scholastica wept and then prayed, and a violent storm with driving rain and hail began. Benedict was forced to stay all night. Back at Monte Cassino a few days later, he had a vision of his sister's death: He saw a white dove fly from her body towards heaven. The twins were buried together when Benedict died. Canonized: By popular acclaim. Feast: February 10.

Stress
St. Walter of Pontnoise (died 1095), France
Little is known about St. Walter's early life in France. Nonetheless, the story of his struggles with stress and a desire to simplify his life is timeless. He was well educated and actively engaged as a professor of philosophy and rhetoric when he saw that some personal changes were needed. So he joined the

Benedictines to find a quiet life of prayer and reflection.

Soon, however, Walter's abilities suggested him as the best candidate for abbot of the abbey at Pontnoise. He was upset. Becoming abbot was a lifelong appointment. He longed to be free of extra responsibilities and work.

Stressed and unhappy, Walter tried to escape from his job. But Pope Gregory XV refused his resignation, and Walter returned to face this unwanted role. For the rest of his life, he dutifully and lovingly fulfilled his responsibilities. Walter became adept at finding silence and relief in quiet corners. Canonized: By popular acclaim. Feast: April 8.

Throat Ailments
St. Blaíse—see *Veterinarians,* p. 92.

Toothaches
St. Apollonia—see *Dentists,* p. 68.

Travelers
St. Christopher—see *Drivers and Transportation Workers,* p. 69.

Volcanoes (Protection From)
St. Agatha—see *Breast Disease,* p. 97.

Weather Dangers
St. Swithun (800–862), England
In England many churches have been named after the beloved St. Swithun. Perhaps that's because St. Swithun's charity was so memorable. Life in ninth-century western England was hard. Without wealth and power, peasants were the first to suffer as victims of abuse, catastrophe, and disease.

Swithun, bishop of Winchester, saw Jesus in every poor and grimy face. On his deathbed he asked to be buried outside, contrary to Church custom for bishops of the day. That way his people could pass over him and the rain could fall upon his grave. Despite his wishes, however, his body was a few years later ceremoniously moved into the cathedral.

Some presumed that Swithun didn't approve, since it rained for forty days after the move. Superstitions rather than miracles were later linked to Swithun's famous connection with the weather:

Saint Swithun's day, if thou dost rain
For forty days it will remain;
Saint Swithun's day, if thou be fair,
For forty days
twill rain no mair.

Canonized: By popular acclaim. Feast: July 15.

Women in Labor
St. Anne—see *Expectant Mothers,* p. 44.

Chapter Five

Patron Saints of Nations and Continents

The Americas (North, South, and Central America)
Our Lady of Guadalupe
Mary came in 1531 to a simple native peasant near Mexico City. The Virgin appeared as an Aztec maiden, asked for a church to be built on the site, and left her image on the cloak of the peasant, Juan Diego. These visions and the cloak helped convert millions from pagan cults that featured human sacrifice and slavery. Pope Pius XII named Our Lady of Guadalupe—as she came to be called in association with this apparition—the Patroness of the Americas in 1945. Feast: December 12.

Angola
The Immaculate Heart of Mary
Among many faithful Catholics, Mary's pure and sinless heart has long been seen as a symbol of her compassion and open arms. The devotion to Mary's Sacred Heart, another expression of her "Immaculate Heart," was first approved in 1805 by Pope Pius VII. So it is a relatively recent devotion.

The apparitions at Fatima a hundred years later further popularized the devotion, since Mary asked for consecration to her Immaculate Heart. Angola was officially put under the patronage of the Immaculate Heart of Mary by the Holy Father, Pope John Paul II, on November 21, 1984.

Argentina
Our Lady of Lujan

In 1630, a twenty-two-inch terra cotta statue of the Immaculate Virgin was sent to Argentina from Brazil. When plans were made to take it to Santiago del Estero, oxen pulling the wagon with the statue refused to cross the Lujan River. That was seen as a sign to make a shrine for the statue nearby.

Chapels were built for the statue and a basilica erected for it in 1887. In that same year, it was covered in silver to help preserve it, leaving only the oval face and hands visible.

Armenia
St. Gregory the Illuminator (257–332), Armenia

Gregory's family had to flee Armenia when he was an infant because his father, Anak, had killed King Khosrov I of that nation. He spent his early life in Caesarea, a city on the Mediterranean that both Sts. Paul and Peter had visited. The young man married, had two sons, and eventually became a bishop.

A wonderful evangelist, Gregory longed to return to Armenia. But when he did, he was imprisoned and tortured for thirteen years by the new king, Khosrov's son. Yet slowly, Gregory's faith converted the king, who then helped him convert Armenia. Canonized: By popular acclaim. Feast: September 30.

Asia Minor
St. John the Apostle (first century), Galilee

The "beloved disciple," as John was called (see Jn 13:23), was one of the twelve apostles and the only one who didn't die a martyr's death. Tradition suggests that John lived in Ephesus in

Asia Minor, caring for the Mother of Jesus. He may have also spent time in Rome in prison.

In Ephesus and on the island of Patmos, John reportedly wrote the Book of Revelation and the fourth Gospel. His residence in this region gave rise to his patronage of Asia Minor. Canonized: By popular acclaim. Feast: December 27.

Australia
Our Lady Help of Christians

Mary has been the favorite patron saint of many peoples and nations. That's because Christians understand her special role as an intercessor. She is the Mother of God and the Mother of the Church. As the Mother of all Christians, she responds to any call for help from her children. In 1964, Pope Paul VI venerated Mary as the patroness of Australia and New Zealand under the title "Our Lady Help of Christians."

Belgium
St. Joseph—see *The Church*, p. 21.

Bohemia
St. Wenceslaus (907–29), St. Ludmilla (d. 927), Bohemia

The oldest son of Duke Ratislav, Wenceslaus was well educated by his grandmother, St. Ludmilla; both are honored as patron saints of Bohemia. The bright boy learned his school subjects well, but he also learned to love his faith. He became the ruler in Bohemia at age fifteen after his father died, then married a few years later and had a son.

Ludmilla was murdered by a pagan political faction that opposed her Christian influence on the throne. Wenceslaus' brother, no longer heir to the throne after the prince was born, joined the opposition party and eventually murdered Wenceslaus on the way to Mass. Many miracles were attributed to the saintly king, especially at his tomb. Canonized: By popular acclaim. Feast: September 28.

Bolivia
Our Lady of Copacabaña
In the late nineteenth century, a statue of the Virgin was fashioned from plaster and wood by native fishermen of Bolivia. The fishermen wanted to thank Mary for her protection. The statue became the object of Marian veneration and was originally housed in a shrine near Lake Titicaca. As devotion to Mary under this title grew, the statue was relocated to a larger church and was crowned in 1925.

Borneo
St. Francis Xavier (1506–52), Spain
Francis, a Basque Spaniard and one of the seven founding Jesuits, had met Ignatius Loyola at the University of Paris. Francis seemed to have been born with a missionary's heart. Beginning in 1540, he served missions in the Far East. Called the "Apostle of the Indies" and the "Apostle of Japan," he died as he attempted to begin mission work in China as well. Borneo later claimed this missionary as its own protector. Canonized: 1622. Feast: December 3.

Brazil
Nossa Senhora Aparecida (Our Lady Who Appeared)
In 1717, three fishermen of Guarantinqueta near São Paulo went out to catch fish for a great feast. The fishermen first

pulled in from the water a statue of the Immaculate Conception. Made about 1650, the three-foot-high painted clay statue had become brown in the river waters of the Paraiba River.

Then the fishermen unexpectedly hauled in a huge catch of fish. It was the first miracle of the *"Virgin Aparecida,"* the "Virgin Who Appeared." During a visit to Brazil, Pope John Paul II named her sanctuary a basilica. Seating seventy thousand, it is the world's largest Marian shrine. Feast: October 12.

Canada
St. Anne—see *Expectant Mothers*, p. 44.

Chile
St. James the Greater—see *Pilgrims and Pilgrimages*, p. 33.

China
St. Joseph—see *The Church*, p. 21.

Colombia
St. Peter Claver—see *Missions Among People of African Descent*, p. 29.

Corsica
The Immaculate Conception
The dogma of the Immaculate Conception is the belief that the Blessed Virgin Mary was preserved from original sin and its consequences from the moment of her conception by a unique act of God's grace. The doctrine was defined by Pope Pius IX in 1854, but the belief had been well rooted in the Church for centuries.

The little island of Corsica, a French territory, has only 250,000 inhabitants. For centuries, the island has been the object of conquest by many invaders. Claiming Mary, the Immaculate Conception, as its protector, Corsica appeals to the sinless, loving Mother of the Redeemer for protection.

Cuba
Our Lady of Charity of El Cobre
While looking for sea salt to preserve meat in 1600, two native Indians and a slave boy found a sixteen-inch painted clay statue of Mary attached to a board and floating in the sea. Mary holds a Child who raises his hand in blessing. She became and remains a national treasure, with the national Cuban shield embroidered on her skirt. In some depictions of Our Lady of Charity, the three men in their small boat are added below her feet. In 1977, her sanctuary in El Cobre was made a basilica.

Czechoslovakia
St. Wenceslaus—see *Bohemia,* p. 115.

Denmark
St. Ansgar (801–65), Denmark
Born in France of a noble family, Ansgar chose religious life as a Benedictine at an early age. He lived at several abbeys and accompanied King Harold of Denmark when the king returned home after exile.

Denmark was largely pagan, and Ansgar, a gifted preacher and evangelist, became the first Christian missionary to Scandinavia. He established the first Christian school in Denmark, but pagans forced him to leave. He returned home and later became archbishop of Bremen. Canonized: By popular acclaim. Feast: February 3.

Dominican Republic
The Virgin of *La Altagracia* (The Virgin of High Grace)

Two brothers from Spain brought a painting of a nativity scene to their new home in the Dominican Republic in the sixteenth century. In the picture, Mary, garbed in a blue cloak sprinkled with stars, gazes at her Child lying on straw in the manger. Mary's image touched the people, and it has been revered ever since in a church—now a basilica—in Higuey.

The image was given a gold and jeweled frame in the eighteenth century and was restored in Spain in 1978. In 1979, Pope John Paul II crowned Our Lady of *La Altagracia* with a gold and silver tiara, his personal gift. Also a patron saint of the Dominican Republic: **St. Dominic**—see *Astronomers*, p. 61.

East Indies
St. Thomas the Apostle—see *Doubters*, p. 23.

Ecuador
The Sacred Heart of Jesus

The patron of this nation is the crucified Christ, whose heart was pierced on the cross. Blood and water poured forth to the earth and remind the world for all time that the Lord gave every drop of blood from his loving heart. Devotion to the Sacred Heart of Jesus began with the messages given to St. Margaret Mary Alacoque (1647-90) before the Blessed Sacrament. Feast: The Friday after the second Sunday after the Solemnity of Pentecost.

El Salvador
Our Lady of Peace
Devotion to Our Lady of Peace began when a mysterious box, which had washed up on a beach, was opened in San Miguel. It was November 21, 1682. Inside was a beautiful wood statue of Our Lady holding the Child.

Salvadorans never forgot her. In 1787, they prayed to Our Lady for protection from the Chaparrastique volcano. The lava changed direction when the statue was displayed. In 1833, the Virgin was invoked to instill peace and a renewed brotherhood after bloody struggles. A new shrine dedicated to Our Lady of Peace was built in 1953, and the nation was placed under her patronage in 1966. Feast: November 21.

England
St. George (died 304), Palestine
Though the more popular components of this saint's story are strictly apocryphal, St. George was likely a soldier who was martyred in Palestine. In later centuries, legends told of his exploits as a knight who saved a maiden from a dragon, worked miracles, and converted thousands to the faith. Crusaders returning to England apparently spread these tales about St. George. By the fifteenth century, the feast of St. George was a major festival and feast in England. Canonized: By popular acclaim. Feast: April 23.

Equatorial Guinea
The Immaculate Conception—see *Corsica*, p. 117. Mary under
the title of the "Immaculate Conception" was named patroness of Equatorial Guinea on May 25, 1986.

Europe
St. Benedict of Nursia—see *Monks*, p. 29.
Sts. Cyril & Methodius—see *Ecumenists*, p. 24.
St. Catherine of Siena—see *Nursing Homes*, p. 50.

St. Bridget of Sweden (1302–73)
Happily married for twenty-eight years, Bridget (or Birgitta) was the mother of eight children, including St. Catherine of Sweden. As a child, Bridget had visions, mostly about the crucified Christ. This devotion never left her, and after the death of her husband Ulf, Bridget founded a religious order, counseled kings and popes, and devotedly served the poor. She died in Rome but her body was returned to her monastery at Vadstena. Canonized: 1391. Feast: July 23.

St. Edith Stein (St. Teresa Benedicta of the Cross) (1891–1942), Germany

On October 1, 1999, Pope John Paul II added three women saints as patrons of Europe. The Holy Father said that he added them to the three male patrons—St. Benedict and Sts. Cyril and Methodius—because they were "connected in a special way to the continent's history."

St. Catherine of Siena was a Dominican tertiary who cared for the poor and the sick and also was a counselor of intellectuals and popes. She became the second woman named as Doctor of the Church. St. Bridget of Sweden was a mystic and prophet who reformed monasteries in the same century in which Catherine lived. Edith Stein, the only modern patron, was a Jewish philosopher who converted to the Catholic faith, became a Carmelite nun, and died at Auschwitz, a Nazi concentration camp, in 1942.

Benedict, the father of Western monasticism, had been named patron saint of Europe in 1964. Cyril and Methodius, missionaries in Moravia, were named patrons in 1980.

Finland
St. Henry of Upsala (died c. 1156), Finland
An Englishman by birth, Henry was an ardent churchman who became bishop of Upsala in Sweden in 1152. He accompanied the Swedish king, St. Eric, on an expedition against Finland and remained in Finland to spread the faith. Henry's alliance with a foreign king may have been resented. He was murdered by a peasant whom he'd excommunicated for murder. Canonized: By popular acclaim. Feast: January 19.

France
St. Joan of Arc—see *Soldiers,* p. 89.
St. Thérèse of Lisieux—see *Foreign Missions,* p. 26. Thérèse was named a special patron of France on May 3, 1944, near the end of World War II.

Germany
St. Boniface (c. 675–755), Germany
Boniface was an English monk who compiled the first Latin grammar written in England. At about age forty, this bookish monk left England to be a missionary among the pagan tribes of Germany. He was wonderfully effective and successful.

The pope made him a bishop and then archbishop of Mainz. At age seventy, Boniface was still active and traveling. In a forest in Friesland, Boniface and his band were martyred by pagans. Canonized: 1874. Feast: June 5. Also a patron of

Germany: **St. Michael the Archangel**—see *Emergency Medical Technicians*, p. 71.

Gibraltar
Our Lady of Europe
A rocky little peninsula of 2.3 square miles juts into the Mediterranean and commands the western entrance to the Mediterranean Sea. This narrow, southernmost tip of the Spanish peninsula has always had strategic importance for Europe. The people of this small nation knew that they needed more than their awesome rock for security and protection. So on May 31, 1979, Gibraltar was placed under Mary's protection under the title "Our Lady of Europe."

Greece
St. Nicholas of Myra—see *Children*, p. 40.

Holland
St. Willibrord (658–739), Holland
Willibrord was an Englishman who studied for the priesthood at Irish monasteries. Then he agreeably became a missionary to pagans in Friesland, Holland. Willibrord was so successful as an evangelist that he became known as the "Apostle to the Frisians" and was named bishop of Utrecht in Holland. In his heart and mind, this missionary truly became one with the people he served for over fifty years. Canonized: By popular acclaim. Feast: November 7.

Hungary
St. Stephen (975–1038), Hungary

At age twenty-six, Stephen became Hungary's first king, with the blessings of the pope. He then used his power to strengthen the Church and help his people. Stephen built new churches and monasteries, assisted the poor, and reorganized the government.

Tragically, Stephen's son and heir was killed in a hunting accident in 1031. In his last years, Stephen had only his faith to strengthen him as he saw others fighting over his throne. Canonized: 1083. Feast: August 16. Also a patron of Hungary: **"Great Lady of Hungary"** (Mary).

Iceland
St. Thorlac (1133–93), Iceland

Thorlac was ordained a priest at age eighteen and then sent to study at Paris and in England. There the young priest saw high standards of ecclesiastical discipline. He also found that European churches were well run.

Thorlac shocked his friends back in Iceland when he refused to marry a wealthy woman. Instead, despite strong opposition, Thorlac labored hard to restore Church discipline. He founded a monastery, instituted reforms, and became the bishop of Skalholt. Named patron saint of Iceland on January 14, 1984. Canonized: By popular acclaim. Feast: December 23.

India
Our Lady of the Assumption

This is a title given to Mary reflecting the dogma that the Virgin was assumed, body and soul, into heaven at the end of her earthly life. That dogma was declared in 1950 and is a source of consolation for all the children of Mary. Devotion to Mary under this title reinforces the hope that we too will one day be fully restored, body and soul. We will be in heaven's glory, enjoying the eternal joy of seeing and living with God. Feast: August 15.

Ireland
St. Patrick—see *Bishops,* p. 15.
Also patrons of Ireland: **St. Brigid (or Bride or Briege)**—see *Nuns,* p. 31; and **St. Columba (c. 521–97), Ireland,** abbot and missionary to Scotland.

Italy
St. Francis of Assisi—see *Catholic Action,* p. 17.
Also a patron saint of Italy: **St. Catherine of Siena**—see *Nursing Homes,* p. 50.

Japan
St. Peter Baptist (1545–97), Spain
A Spanish Franciscan missionary, Peter had a burning desire to serve in the foreign missions. He led a group of missionaries to Japan, where they were joined by the Jesuit Fr. Paul Miki and a Korean layman, Leo Karasuma. Feelings in Japan towards the foreign missionaries had been no more than tolerant. When the political climate deteriorated, the missionaries were arrested, crucified, and stabbed to death in Nagasaki. Canonized: 1862. Feast: February 6.

Korea
St. Joseph—see *The Church,* p. 21.

Lesotho
The Immaculate Heart of Mary—see *Angola*, p. 113.

Lithuania
St. Casimir (1458–84), Poland
In many ways, Casimir, the third child of Polish King Casimir IV, didn't fit in. He disliked the pomp and fancy clothes at court and gave his own things to the poor. Still, Casimir was obedient. He even agreed to become Hungary's king when Hungarian nobles pressured the fifteen-year-old to take the crown.

Disgusted by politics and the abuse of power, Casimir eventually abandoned public life for a monastic life. He died at age twenty-six of consumption and was buried holding a copy of his favorite Marian hymn. Canonized: 1522. Feast: March 4. Also a patron of Lithuania: **Blessed Cunegunda (1224–92), Poland,** Franciscan tertiary and wife of Boleslaus V, King of Poland.

Luxembourg
St. Willibrord—see *Holland*, p. 123.

Malta
St. Paul (died 67), Tarsus, Asia Minor
A Jew and Roman citizen, Paul was born in Tarsus in Cilicia. A well-educated Pharisee, he persecuted Christians until Jesus confronted him on the road to Damascus. From then on, he was the "Apostle to the Gentiles" and the most prolific author of the New Testament.

Paul evangelized in Cyprus, Greece, and throughout Asia Minor. He was shipwrecked near Malta. Paul was beheaded in Rome for his faith. Canonized: By popular acclaim. Feasts (with St. Peter): June 29; Conversion, January 25. Also a patron saint of Malta: **Our Lady of the Assumption**—see *India,* p. 124.

Mexico
Our Lady of Guadalupe—see The *Americas,* p. 111.

Monaco
St. Devota (died 303), Corsica

This strong young Christian woman was born on the island of Corsica. She was arrested for her faith during the persecution of Christians under Diocletian. Dragged through the streets, she was then tortured and killed on the rack as she steadily refused to deny Christ.

As Devota's body was being taken home by boat, a fierce storm threatened the vessel and a dove appeared and guided it to Monaco. Devota was buried there. Canonized: By popular acclaim. Feast: January 27.

Moravia
Sts. Cyril and Methodius—see *Ecumenists,* p. 24.

New Zealand
Our Lady Help of Christians

This title of Our Lady reflects devotion to Mary as a powerful intercessor before her Son, Jesus Christ. Because she is the Mother of the Church as well as the Mother of God, she is indeed the Help of Christians. Mary longs to assist her sons and daughters. She is a fitting patron for an island nation evangelized mainly by the Marists.

Norway
St. Olaf II (995–1030), Norway

Soon after he was killed in battle at age thirty-five, stories about St. Olaf grew larger than life. But he was a truly remarkable leader, king, and Christian. He became the first king of a united Norway and was aggressive about instituting Christianity.

Some Norwegian nobles resented Olaf, and he was dethroned and exiled for two years. When he returned to regain his kingdom, he was outnumbered and killed. Olaf's blood reportedly healed the wound of Tore Hund, who had speared the king. Within two years after his murder, Olaf was heralded as a saint and the "Eternal King of Norway." Canonized: 1164. Feast: July 29.

Papua New Guinea and the Northern Solomon Islands
St. Michael the Archangel—see *Emergency Medical Technicians*, p. 71.

St. Michael was named the patron saint of Papua New Guinea on May 31, 1979.

Paraguay
Our Lady of the Assumption—see *India*, p. 124.

Our Lady of the Assumption was named the patron saint of Paraguay on July 13, 1951.

Peru
St. Joseph—see *The Church*, p. 21.

St. Joseph was named the patron saint of Peru on March 19, 1957.

The Philippines
The Sacred Heart of Mary

Another expression of devotion to the Immaculate Heart of Mary. Among many faithful Catholics, Mary's pure and sinless heart has long been seen as a symbol of her compassion and open arms. The devotion to Mary's Sacred Heart was first approved in 1805 by Pope Pius VII, so it is a relatively recent devotion. The apparitions at Fatima a hundred years later further popularized the devotion, since Mary asked for consecration to her Sacred Heart. It is a favorite devotion in the Philippines.

Poland
St. Casimir—see *Lithuania*, p. 123.

Also patron saints of Poland: **Blessed Cunegunda**—see *Lithuania*, p. 123; **St. Stanislaus of Krakow (1030–79),** bishop and martyr; **Our Lady of Czesthochowa.**

Portugal
The Immaculate Conception—see *Corsica*, p. 117.

Also patron saints of Portugal: **St. Francis Borgia (1510–72), Spain,** father general of the Jesuits; **St. Anthony of Padua**—see *Lost Items*, p. 107; **St. Vincent of Saragossa (died 304),** deacon and martyr; **St. George**—see *England*, p. 120.

Russia
St. Nicholas of Myra—see *Children*, p. 40.

Also a patron saint of Russia: **St. Andrew**—see *Scotland*, p. 130.

Scandinavia
St. Ansgar—see *Denmark,* p. 118.

Scotland
St. Andrew the Apostle (first century), Galilee
Andrew was the first apostle to follow Jesus. But Andrew also led people to Jesus, including his own brother Peter. After the death and resurrection of Jesus, Andrew reportedly went to evangelize in Achaia, the Roman name for Greece.

Later accounts say that Andrew was martyred there, crucified on an X-shaped cross, and that he preached from his cross for two days before dying. An old legend suggests that St. Rule or Regulus took Andrew's relics to Scotland in the fourth century. Canonized: By popular acclaim. Feast: November 30. Also a patron saint of Scotland: **St. Columba**—see *Ireland,* p. 125.

Slovakia
Our Lady of Sorrows
This is a devotion to Mary based on her trials and grief as the Mother of Jesus. The Savior was destined to die to redeem the world. Mary's sorrows were related to this destiny.

The sorrows included events from Jesus' childhood, such as the ominous prophecy of Simeon, the hurried flight into Egypt, and the slaughter of the innocent children. Other sorrows were events of her Son's passion and death in Jerusalem. Devotion to the "Seven Sorrows of Mary" developed in the Middle Ages. Feast: September 15.

The Solomon Islands
The Most Holy Name of Mary
A devotion founded on the understanding that Mary's holiness

was a gift to her because she was to be the Mother of Jesus, the Son of God. Mary is the appropriate recipient of honor but not worship. This traditional devotion to and affection for the name of Mary was formally approved in the Solomon Islands of the Pacific on September 6, 1991.

South Africa
Our Lady of the Assumption—see *India,* p. 124.
Our Lady of the Assumption was named the patron saint of South Africa on March 15, 1952.

South America
St. Rose of Lima (1586–1617), Peru
Beautiful St. Rose is a particularly fitting patron for her continent. She was the first person born in the Americas to be canonized. Like St. Catherine of Siena, whom she emulated, Rose lived at home as a Dominican tertiary.

Rose tirelessly served the poor and sick of Lima. She raised flowers to sell and did needlework for pay. She prayed, did penance, and put off suitors by marring her face with pepper and lye. Rose died at age thirty-one. Canonized: 1671. Feast: August 23.

Spain
St. Teresa of Avila—see *Headache Sufferers,* p. 105.
Also a patron saint of Spain: **St. James the Greater**—see *Pilgrims and Pilgrimages,* p. 33.

Sri Lanka (Ceylon)
St. Lawrence (died 258), Rome

An archdeacon for the Church in Rome, Lawrence was temporarily spared execution with orders to gather Church money and treasures so that he could surrender them to the imperial authorities. On August 6, the pope and six deacons were beheaded. Lawrence arrived August 10 for his execution with poor and handicapped people. He explained that they were "the true treasure of the Church." Lawrence was burned to death on a gridiron and defied his torturers with jokes about being "done on one side." Canonized: By popular acclaim. Feast: August 10.

Sweden
St. Bridget of Sweden —see Europe, p. 121. Also a patron saint of Sweden: St. Eric (died 1160), Sweden, king and supporter of the Church.

Tanzania
The Immaculate Conception—see *Corsica,* p. 117.

The Immaculate Conception was named as patron saint of Tanzania on December 8, 1964.

The United States
The Immaculate Conception—see *Corsica,* p. 117.

In 1846, the U.S. bishops asked the pope to name the Virgin Mary as the patroness for the United States under her title "the Immaculate Conception." The United States was still a young nation—just seventy years old. The American bishops knew that this new country was already facing many large challenges. Immigrants were pouring into America from many different lands. The United States needed a special patron, an understanding Mother who would watch over and protect this land with citizens from so many different cultures.

In 1847, the bishops began to plan a national shrine dedicated to the Immaculate Conception in Washington, D.C. Seven years later, Pope Pius IX declared that Mary's sinlessness from conception was to be a doctrine of faith. In the United States, Americans may have felt that their patron saint had been fortuitously assigned. The United States, which many immigrants saw as an unstained "promised land of freedom," had chosen as a protector the pure Mother of the promised Redeemer, Jesus.

Uruguay
La Virgen de los Treinte y Tres (The Virgin of the Thirty-Three)

Around 1779, a wood statue of the Assumption of Mary, which had been carved in Paraguay, was relocated to the city of Florida, Uruguay. In 1825, thirty-three Uruguayan patriots committed to independence for Uruguay prayed before the statue, asking the Virgin to bless their efforts. Later, they placed their newborn nation under her protection. In 1961, the statue received an oversized gold and jeweled crown. Pope John XXIII named her the patroness of Uruguay. Feast: Second Sunday of November.

Venezuela
Our Lady of Coromoto

In 1651, about fifty years after the Spanish arrived near Guanare bringing the Christian faith, a Coromoto Indian chief and his wife were visited by Our Lady and her Child. She urged them to take their people to receive baptism, "the water on the head," in order to enter heaven. The chief stubbornly resisted the beautiful lady until she left a small holy card with her image in his clenched fist. That tiny card is kept in a monstrance in the National Sanctuary of the Virgin of Coromoto. Feasts: February 2, September 8 and 11.

Vietnam
Our Lady of La Vang
In 1798, Our Lady reportedly appeared to frightened Christians fleeing persecution in the La Vang Forest near Hue. Christians often hid near a large banyan tree there. Our Lady appeared with a long cape, held the Christ child, and was flanked by two angels. She consoled them and told them to boil leaves from surrounding trees as a medicine.

Villagers later built a platform and fence around the area, and a thatched roof temple was given to Catholics in the 1820s. The shrine was often destroyed—most recently during the Vietnam War. Pope John XXIII declared the shrine a cathedral. A hundred thousand pilgrims visited during the two hundredth anniversary in 1998. Feast: August 15.

Wales
St. David (died 589), Wales
Dewi Sant is Welsh for "St. David," a beloved name for centuries in Wales. According to legend, this son of a Cardigan chieftain became a priest and went on pilgrimage to Jerusalem. He returned a bishop and founded a monastery near Pembroke.

David's monks were very strict, abstaining even from wine. He evangelized much of southern Wales, and at least fifty places were dedicated to him there. Canonized: 1220. Feast: March 1.

West Indies
St. Gertrude the Great (1256–1302), Germany

Deep devotion to Gertrude in the West Indies may be the reason for her patronage there. She never went to the Indies and probably never ventured far from the Cistercian convent at Helfta in Saxony where she was taken as an orphan at age five.

A brilliant child, she mastered every subject until a vision of Christ rebuked her. Later, she studied only Scripture and the Church Fathers. A mystic and visionary, she wrote prolifically, spreading devotion to the Sacred Heart. She has not been formally canonized, but her feast was declared in 1677. Feast: November 16.

Index by Patron Saint's Name

For Saints with multiple listings, biographical information can be found in the first entry listed.

~ A ~

St. Adjutor – Swimmers, 90; Drowning Danger, 101

St. Agatha – Breast Disease, 97; Volcanoes (Protection from), 111

St. Albert the Great – Scientists, 87

Sts. Alodia and Nunilo – Child Abuse, 99; Runaways and Missing Persons, 109

St. Aloysius Gonzaga – Youth, 55; AIDS Patients and Ministers, 95

St. Alphonsus Liguori – Confessors, 21; Vocations, 38

St. Andrew – Scotland, 130; Russia, 129

St. Anne – Expectant Mothers, 44; Grandmothers, 46; Women in Labor, 112; Canada, 117

St. Ansgar – Denmark, 118; Scandinavia, 130

St. Anthony of Padua – Lost Items, 107; Poverty, 108; Portugal, 129

St. Anthony the Great - Hermits, 27

St. Apollonia – Dentists, p. 68; Toothaches, 111

St. Augustine – Theologians, 38

~ B ~

St. Bede the Venerable – Scholars, 86

St. Benedict of Nursia – Monks, 29; Poison Protection, 108; Europe, 121

St. Benedict Joseph Labre – The Homeless, 106

St. Bernard of Methon – Mountain Climbers, 80; Skiers, 88

St. Bernard the Navigator – Sailors, 85

St. Bernardine of Siena – Advertisers, Communications and Public Relations Personnel, 58

St. Bernward – Architects, 59

St. Blaíse – Veterinarians, 92 ; Throat Ailments, 9, 111

St. Bonaventure – Bowel or Intestinal Disorders, 96

St. Boniface – Germany, 122-23

St. Brigid of Ireland – Nuns, 31; Dairy Workers, 68; Ireland, 125

St. Bridget of Sweden – Europe, 10, 121; Sweden, 132

St. Brendan the Navigator – Sailors, 85-86

~ C ~

St. Camillus de Lellis – Nurses, 81; Gambling, 9, 104; the Sick, 110

St. Casimir – Lithuania, 126; Poland, 129

St. Catherine of Siena – Nursing Homes, 50; Europe, 10, 121-22; Italy, 125

St. Cecilia – Composers, Musicians, and Singers, 66

St. Charles Borromeo – Seminarians, 37

St. Charles Lwanga – Converts, 22

St. Christopher – Drivers and Transportation Workers, 69-70; Travelers, 111

St. Clare – Television Writers and Television, 91-92

St. Columba – Ireland, p. 125; Scotland, 139

Bl. Cunegunda – Lithuania, p. 126; Poland, 129

Sts. Cyril & Methodius – Ecumenists, p. 24; Europe, 10, 121; Moravia, 127

~ D ~

St. (Pope) Damasus I – Archaeologists, 59

St. David, King of Israel – Poets, 84

St. David of Wales – Wales, 134

St. Devota – Monaco, 127

St. Dismas – Death Row Inmates, 100

St. Dominic – Astronomers, 12, 61-62

Bl. Dorothy of Montau – Miscarriage and Stillborn Infants, 48-49

~ E ~

St. Edith Stein – Europe, p. 10, 121-22

St. Eligius – Jewelers and Metal Workers, p. 76-77

St. Elizabeth Ann Seton – Grieving Parents, p. 46; Single Parents, p. 52

St. Elizabeth of Hungary – Young Brides, p. 54; Bakers, p. 63

St. Eric – Sweden, p.121

St. Eugene de Mazenod – Dysfunctional or Hurting Families, p. 43-44

~ F ~

St. (King) Ferdinand III – Tertiaries or Third Order Members, 37-38 ; Engineers, 71

St. Fiacre – Cabdrivers, 65

St. Florian – Firefighters, 72; Fire Danger, 104

Blessed Fra Angelico – Artists, 60-61

St. Frances Xavier Cabrini – Hospital Administrators, 75; Emigrants, 101; Refugees, 109

St. Francis de Sales – Catholic Press, 18-19; Authors, Journalists, and Writers, 63; Deafness and Hearing Disorders, 100

St. Francis of Assisi – Catholic Action, 17-18; Ecologists, 70; Merchants and Sales Personnel, 95; Animals, 95; Italy, 125

St. Francis of Paola – Naval Officers and Personnel, 80-81

St. Francis Xavier – Borneo, 116

~ G ~

St. Gabriel the Archangel – Broadcasters, 63-64; Diplomats, 69; Postal Employees, 84; Telecommunications Workers, 91

St. Gemma Galgani – Pharmacists, 82-83

St. Genesius of Arles – Secretaries and Clerks, 87-88

St. Genesius the Actor – Actors and Actresses, 57-58

St. George – England, 120; Portugal, 129

St. Gerard Majella – Childbirth, 39-40

St. Germaine Cousin – Handicapped People, 105

St. Gertrude the Great – West Indies, 134-35

St. Gottschalk – Linguists, 78-79

St. Gregory Illuminator – Armenia, 114

St. Gregory the Great – Popes, 33-34

St. Guy of Anderlecht – Sacristans, 36

~ H ~

St. Helena – Divorced Women and Men, 43
St. Henry of Upsala – Finland, 122-23
St. Heribert – Drought, 101
St. Homobonus Tucingo – Business Professionals, 64-65
St. Hubert – Hunters, 76

~ I ~

St. Ignatius of Loyola – Retreats, 35-36
The Immaculate Conception – Corsica, 117-18; Equatorial Guinea, 120; Portugal, 129; Tanzania, 132; the United States, 132-33
The Immaculate Heart of Mary – Angola, 113; Lesotho, 126
St. Isidore of Seville – Computer and Internet Users, 9, 66-67
St. Isidore the Farmer - Farmers, 71-72
St. Ivo or Yves – Lawyers, 77

~ J ~

St. James the Greater – Pilgrims and Pilgrimages, 33; Arthritis and Rheumatism, 95; Chile, 117; Spain, 131
St. Jane Frances de Chantal – In-Law Conflicts, 48; Widows, 54
St. Januarius – Bleeding, 95-96
St. Jean-Baptist de la Salle – Teachers, 91
St. Jean-Baptiste Vianney – Priests, 35
St. Jerome – Librarians, 77-78
St. Jerome Emiliani – Orphans, 50-51
St. Joachim – Grandfathers, 45-46
St. Joan of Arc – Soldiers, 89-90; France, 122
St. John, Apostle – Friendship, 26-27; Publishers, 85; Asia Minor, 114-15
St. John Berchmans - Altar Servers, 15
St. John Bosco – Editors, 70
St. John Capistran - Chaplains, Military Chaplains, 19-20
St. John Chrysostom — Preachers, 34; Orators and Public Speakers, 81
St. John Gualbert – Forestry and Park Workers, 73

St. John Nepomuk – Floods, 104

St. John of God – Printers, 85; Alcoholism, 95; Heart Disease and Ailments, 106

St. John of the Cross – Mystics, 30-31

St. John Regis – Medical Workers, 79

St. Joseph – The Church, 21; Fathers, 44; Carpenters, 65; Workers, 93; The Dying, 102; Belgium, 115; China, 117; Korea, 125; Peru, 128

St. Joseph Cafasso – Prisoners, 108-109

St. Joseph Moscati – Single Men, 52

St. Joseph of Arimathea – Funeral Directors, 73-74

St. Joseph of Cupertino – Astronauts and Pilots, 9, 61

St. Jude Thaddeus – Desperate Situations or Needs, 100-101

St. Justin – Philosophers, 83

~ L ~

St. Lawrence – Sri Lanka, 132

St. Leonard of Port Maurice – Parish Missions, 32

St. (King) Leopold – Stepparents, 53

St. Lidwina of Schiedham – Skaters, 88

St. (King) Louis IX – Parents of Large Families , 51-52

St. Louise de Marillac – Social Workers, 89

St. Ludmilla Bohemia, 115-16

St. Luke the Evangelist – Painters, 82; Physicians and Surgeons, 84

~ M ~

St. Marguerite d'Youville – Difficult or Hurting Marriages, 42; Grieving Children, 46

St. Margaret of Cortona – Single Women, 52-53; Midwives, 79

St. Maria Goretti – Rape and Sexual Exploitation, 109

St. Martha – Cooks, 41; Cooks and Chefs, 67

St. Martin de Porres – Interracial Justice and Ministry, 28; Barbers and Hairdressers, 63

St. Martin of Tours – Horsemen and Horsewomen, 74-75; Hotel Personnel, 75

St. Matthew the Apostle – Accountants and Bankers, 57

St. Maximilian Kolbe – Drug Addiction, 102; Political Prisoners, 108

St. Michael the Archangel – Emergency Medical Technicians, 71; Law Enforcement Personnel, 77; Paratroopers, 82; Battle Danger, 95; Germany, 123; Papua New Guinea and the Northern Solomon Islands, 128

St. Monica – Mothers, 46-50

The Most Holy Name of Mary – The Solomon Islands, 130-31

~ N ~

St. Nicholas of Myra – Children, 40-41; Greece, 123; Russia, 129

St. Nicholas von Flue – Council Members and Legislators, 67

Nossa Señora de Aparecida (Our Lady Who Appeared) – Brazil, 116-17

~ O ~

St. Odilia – Blindness and Eye Diseases, 96

St. (King) Olaf II – Norway, 128

St. Osmund – Mental Illness, 107

Our Lady Help of Christians – Australia, 115; New Zealand, 127

Our Lady of Charity of El Cobre – Cuba, 118

Our Lady of Copacabaña – Bolivia, 116

Our Lady of Coromot – Venezuela, 133-34

Our Lady of Europe – Gibraltar, 123

Our Lady of Guadalupe – The Americas, 113; Mexico, 127

Our Lady of La Vang – Vietnam, 134

Our Lady of Lujan – Argentina, 114

Our Lady of Peace – El Salvador, 120

Our Lady of Sorrows – Slovakia, 130

Our Lady of the Assumption – India, 124-125; Malta, 127; Paraguay, 128; South Africa, 131

~ P ~

St. Paschal Baylon – Eucharistic Congresses and Movements, 24-25

St. Patrick – Bishops, 15; Snakes (Protection from) , 110; Ireland, 125

St. Paul, Apostle to the Gentiles – Malta, 126-27

St. Peregrine – Cancer, 98-99

St. Peter the Apostle – The Papacy, 31-32; Fishermen, 72

St. Peter Baptist – Japan, 125

St. Peter Claver – Missions Among People of African Descent, 29; Colombia, 117

St. Philip Howard – Falsely Accused Persons, 103-104

St. Phocas the Gardener – Gardeners, 45, 74

St. Polycarp – Earaches and Ear Ailments, 102-103

~ R ~

St. Raymond of Peñafort – Canon Lawyers, 16

St. Rita of Cascia – Infertile Couples, 13, 47-48

St. Robert Bellarmine – Catechists, 17

St. Rose of Lima – South America, 131

~ S ~

St. Sabas – Lectors, 28-29

The Sacred Heart of Jesus – Ecuador, 119

The Sacred Heart of Mary – Philippines, 129

St. Scholastica – Storm Protection, 110

St. Sebastian – Athletes, 62

St. Stanislaus Kstoka – Broken Bones, 98

St. Stephen – Deacons, 23-23

St. Stephen of Hungary – Hungary, 124

St. Swithun – Weather Dangers, 111

~ T ~

St. Tarsicius – First Communicants, 25

St. Teresa Benedicta of the Cross (*see St. Edith Stein*), 121-22, 10

St. Teresa of Avila – Headache Sufferers, 105-106 Spain, 131

St. Teresa of Jesus of the Andes – Young Women, 55

St. Thérèse of Lisieux – Foreign Missions, 26; Aviators, 63, Florists, 73;
    France, 122, 12, 15

St. Thomas, Apostle – Doubters, 23; East Indies, 119

St. Thomas Aquinas – Catholic Schools, 19; Students, 54, 90

St. Thomas More – Adoptive Families, 39; Widowers, 54; Politicians,
    10, 84

St. Thorlac – Iceland, 124

~ V ~

St. Valentine – Couples in Love, 41-42

St. Vincent de Paul – Charitable Organizations, 20

St. Vincent Ferrer – Builders, Construction Workers, and Plumbers, 64

La Virgen de los Treinte y Tres (The Virgin of the Thirty-Three) – Uruguay,
    133

The Virgin of *La Altagracia* (The Virgin of High Grace) – Dominican
    Republic, 119

St. Vitus – Dancers, 68; Epilepsy, 103

~ W ~

St. Walter of Pontnoise – Stress, 110

St. Wenceslaus – Bohemia, 115-116; Czechoslovakia, 118

St. Willibrord – Holland, 123-24; Luxembourg, 126

~ Z ~

St. Zita – Housekeepers, 47; Housekeepers and Maids, 75

Index by Patronage of Work, Association, Institution, Need, or Place

Few patronages have been officially designated by the Church; most stem from popular tradition. When a patronage has been formally declared by the Church, the date of the declaration is noted.

~ A ~

Accountants and Bankers – St. Matthew the Apostle, 57

Actors and Actresses – St. Genesius the Actor, 57-58

Adoptive Families – St. Thomas More, 39

Advertisers, Communications and Public Relations Personnel – St. Bernardine of Siena (May 20, 1960), 58-59

AIDS Patients and Ministers – St. Aloysius Gonzaga, 95

Alcoholism – St. John of God, 95

Altar Servers – St. John Berchmans, 15

The Americas – Our Lady of Guadalupe, 113

Angola – The Immaculate Heart of Mary (Nov. 21, 1984), 113

Animals – St. Francis of Assisi, 17-18

Archaeologists – St. (Pope) Damasus I, 59

Architects – St. Bernward, 59-60

Argentina – Our Lady of Lujan, 114

Armenia – St. Gregory the Illuminator, 114

Arthritis and Rheumatism – St. James the Greater, 33

Artists –Blessed Fra Angelico, (Feb. 21, 1984), 60-61

Asia Minor – St. John the Apostle, 114-115

Astronauts and Pilots – St. Joseph of Cupertino, 9, 61

Astronomers – St. Dominic, 61-62

Athletes – St. Sebastian, 62

Australia – Our Lady Help of Christians, 115

Authors, Journalists, and Writers – St. Francis de Sales, 63

Aviators –St. Thérèse of Lisieux, 63

~ B ~

Bakers – St. Elizabeth of Hungary, 63

Barbers and Hairdressers – St. Martin de Porres, 63

Battle Danger – St. Michael the Archangel, 95

Belgium – St. Joseph, 115

Bishops – St. Patrick, 15

Bleeding – St. Januarius, 95-96

Blindness and Eye Diseases – St. Odilia, 96

Bohemia – St. Wenceslaus, St. Ludmilla, 115-16

Bolivia – Our Lady of Copacabaña, 116

Borneo – St. Francis Xavier, 116

Bowel or Intestinal Disorders – St. Bonaventure, 96-97

Brazil – *Nossa Señora de Aparecida* (Our Lady Who Appeared), 116-17

Breast Disease – St. Agatha, 97-98

Broadcasters (Radio and Television) – St. Gabriel the Archangel, 63-64

Broken Bones – St. Stanislaus Kostka, 98

Builders, Construction Workers, and Plumbers – St.Vincent Ferrer, 64

Business Professionals – St. Homobonus Tucingo, 64-65

~ C ~

Cabdrivers – St. Fiacre, 65

Canada – St. Anne, 107

Cancer – St. Peregrine, 98-99

Canon Lawyers - St. Raymond of Peñafort, 16

Carpenters – St. Joseph, 65

Catechists – St. Robert Bellarmine, 17

Catholic Action – St. Francis of Assisi (1916), 17-18

Catholic Press – St. Francis de Sales, 18-19

Catholic Schools – St. Thomas Aquinas (Aug. 4, 1880), 19

Chaplains – St. John Capistran, 19-20

Charitable Organizations - St. Vincent de Paul (May 12, 1885), 20

Child Abuse – Sts. Alodia and Nunilo, 99

Childbirth – St. Gerard Majella, 39-40

Children – St. Nicholas of Myra, 40-41

Chile – St. James the Greater, 117

China – St. Joseph, 117

The Church – St. Joseph (Dec. 8, 1970), 21

Colombia – St. Peter Claver, 117

Composers, Musicians, and Singers – St. Cecilia, 66

Computer and Internet Users – St. Isidore of Seville, 66-67

Confessors – St. Alphonsus Liguori (April 26, 1950), 21-22

Converts – St. Charles Lwanga, 22

Cooks and Chefs – St. Martha, 41, 67

Corsica – The Immaculate Conception, 117-18

Council Members and Legislators – St. Nicholas von Flue, 67

Couples in Love – St. Valentine, 41-42

Cuba – Our Lady of Charity of El Cobre, 118

Czechoslovakia – St. Wenceslaus, 118

~ **D** ~

Dairy Workers – St. Brigid of Ireland, 68

Dancers – St. Vitus, 68

Deacons – St. Stephen, 22-23

Deafness and Hearing Disorders – St. Frances de Sales, 100

Death Row Inmates – St. Dismas, 100

Denmark – St. Ansgar, 118-119

Dentists – St. Apollonia, 68-69

Desperate Situations or Needs – St. Jude Thaddeus, 100-101

Difficult or Hurting Marriages – St. Marguerite d'Youville, 42

Diplomats – St. Gabriel the Archangel, 69

Divorced Women and Men – St. Helena, 43

Dominican Republic – The Virgin of *La Altagracia* (The Virgin of High Grace), St. Dominic, 119

Doubters – St. Thomas the Apostle, 23

Drivers and Transportation Workers – St. Christopher, 69-70

Drought – St. Heribert, 101

Drowning Danger – St. Adjutor, 101

Drug Addiction – St. Maximilian Kolbe, 102

The Dying – St. Joseph, 102

Dysfunctional or Hurting Families – St. Eugene de Mazenod, 43-44

~ E ~

Earaches and Ear Ailments – St. Polycarp, 102-103

East Indies – St. Thomas the Apostle, 119

Ecologists – St. Francis of Assisi (Nov. 29, 1979), 70

Ecuador – The Sacred Heart of Jesus, 119

Ecumenists – Sts. Cyril and Methodius, 24

Editors – St. John Bosco, 70

El Salvador – Our Lady of Peace (Oct. 10, 1966), 120

Emergency Medical Technicians – St. Michael the Archangel, 71

Emigrants – St. Frances Xavier Cabrini (Sept. 8, 1950), 103

Engineers – St. (King) Ferdinand III, 71

England – St. George, 120

Epilepsy – St. Vitus, 103

Equatorial Guinea – The Immaculate Conception (May 25, 1986), 120

Eucharistic Congresses and Movements - St. Paschal Baylon (Nov. 28, 1897), 24-25

Europe – St. Benedict of Nursia (1964), p. xx; Sts. Cyril and Methodius (Dec. 31, 1980), St. Catherine of Siena, St. Bridget of Sweden, St. Edith Stein, (Oct. 1, 1999), 10, 121-22

Expectant Mothers – St. Anne, 44

~ F ~

Falsely Accused Persons – St. Philip Howard, 103-104

Farmers – St. Isidore the Farmer, 71-72

Fathers – St. Joseph, 44

Finland – St. Henry of Upsala, 122-23

Fire Danger – St. Florian, 104

Firefighters – St. Florian, 72

First Communicants - St. Tarsicius, 25

Fishermen – St. Peter the Apostle, 72

Florists – St. Thérèse of Lisieux, 26

Floods (Dangers of) – St. John Nepomuk, 104

Foreign Missions – St. Thérèse of Lisieux, 26

Forestry and Park Workers – St. John Gualbert, 73

France –St. Joan of Arc, p. xx; St. Thérèse of Lisieux (May 3, 1944), 122

Friendship – St. John the Apostle, 26-27

Funeral Directors – St. Joseph of Arimathea, 73-74

~ G ~

Gambling – St. Camillus de Lellis, 9, 105

Gardeners – St. Phocas the Gardener, 74

Germany – St. Boniface, 122-23; St. Michael the Archangel, 123

Gibraltar – Our Lady of Europe (May 31, 1979), 123

Grandfathers – St. Joachim, 45-46

Grandmothers – St. Anne, 44

Greece – St. Nicholas of Myra, 123

Grieving Children – St. Marguerite d'Youville, 46

Grieving Parents – St. Elizabeth Ann Seton, 46

~ H ~

The Handicapped – St. Germaine Cousin, 105

Headache Sufferers – St. Teresa of Avila, 105-106

Heart Disease and Ailments – St. John of God, 106

Hermits - St. Anthony the Great, 27

Holland – St. Willibrord, 123-24

The Homeless – St. Benedict Joseph Labre, 106-107

Horsemen and Horsewomen – St. Martin of Tours, 74-75

Hospital Administrators – St. Frances Xavier Cabrini, 75

Hotel Personnel – St. Martin of Tours, 75

Housekeepers and Maids – St. Zita, 75
Hungary – St. Stephen of Hungary, p. xx; "Great Lady of Hungary," 124
Hunters – St. Hubert, 76

~ I ~

Iceland – St. Thorlac (Jan. 14, 1984), 124
India – Our Lady of the Assumption, 124-25
Infertile Couples – St. Rita of Cascia, 13, 47-48
In-Law Conflicts – St. Jane Frances de Chantal, 48
Interracial Justice and Ministry – St. Martin de Porres, 28
Ireland – St. Patrick, 15, St. Brigid (or Bride or Briege), 31, St. Columba, 125
Italy – St. Francis of Assisi, St. Catherine of Siena, 125

~ J ~

Japan – St. Peter Baptist, 125
Jewelers – St. Eligius, 76-77
Journalists – St. Francis de Sales (April 26, 1923), 63

~ K ~

Korea – St. Joseph, p. xx

~ L ~

Law Enforcement Personnel – St. Michael the Archangel, 77
Lawyers – St. Ivo or Yves, 77
Lectors – St. Sabas, 28-29
Lesotho – The Immaculate Heart of Mary, 126
Librarians – St. Jerome, 77-78
Linguists – St. Gottschalk, 78-79
Lithuania – St. Casimir, Bl. Cunegunda, 126
Lost Items – St. Anthony of Padua, 107
Luxembourg – St. Willibrord, 126

~ M ~

Malta – St. Paul, Apostle to the Gentiles, Our Lady of the Assumption, 127

Medical Workers – St. John Regis, 79

Mental Illness – St. Osmund, 108

Merchants and Sales Personnel – St. Francis of Assisi, 79

Metal Workers – St. Eligius, 76-77

Mexico – Our Lady of Guadalupe, 127

Midwives – St. Margaret of Cortona, 79

Military Chaplains – St. John Capistran (Feb. 10, 1984), 19-20

Miscarriage and Stillborn Infants – Blessed Dorothy of Montau, 48-49

Missions Among People of African Descent – St. Peter Claver (1896, Leo XIII), 29

Monaco – St. Devota, 127

Monks - St. Benedict of Nursia, 29-30

Moravia – Sts. Cyril and Methodius, 127

Mothers – St. Monica, 49-50

Mountain Climbers – St. Bernard of Methon, 80

Mystics – St. John of the Cross, 30-31

~ N ~

Naval Officers and Personnel – St. Francis of Paola, 80-81

New Zealand – Our Lady Help of Christians, 127

Norway – St. (King) Olaf II, 128

Nuns – St. Brigid of Ireland, 31

Nurses – St. Camillus de Lellis, 81

Nursing Homes – St. Catherine of Siena, 50

~ O ~

Orators and Public Speakers – St. John Chrysostom (July 8, 1908), 81

Orphans – St. Jerome Emiliani, 50-51

~ P ~

Painters – St. Luke the Evangelist, 82

The Papacy - St. Peter the Apostle, 31-32

Papua New Guinea and the Northern Solomon Islands – St. Michael the Archangel (May 31, 1979), 128

Paraguay – Our Lady of the Assumption (July 13, 1951), 128

Paratroopers – St. Michael the Archangel, 82

Parents of Large Families – St. (King) Louis IX, 51-52

Parish Missions – St. Leonard of Port Maurice (March 17, 1923), 32

Peru – St. Joseph (March 19, 1957), 128

Pharmacists – St. Gemma Galgani, 82-83

The Philippines – The Sacred Heart of Mary, 129

Philosophers – St. Justin, 83

Physicians and Surgeons – St. Luke the Evangelist, 84

Pilgrims and Pilgrimages – St. James the Greater, 33

Poets – St. David, King of Israel, 84

Poison Protection – St. Benedict of Nursia, 108

Poland – St. Casimir, Bl. Cunegunda, St. Stanislaus of Krakow, Our Lady of Czesthochowa, 129

Political Prisoners – St. Maximilian Kolbe, 108

Politicians – St. Thomas More (2000), 84

Popes – St. Gregory the Great, 33-34

Portugal – The Immaculate Conception, St. Francis Borgia, St. Anthony of Padua, St. Vincent of Saragossa, St. George, 129

Postal Employees – St. Gabriel the Archangel, 63-64

Poverty – St. Anthony of Padua, 108

Preachers – St. John Chrysostom, 34

Priests – St. Jean-Baptiste Vianney (April 23, 1929), 35

Printers – St. John of God, 85

Prisoners – St. Joseph Cafasso, 108-109

Publishers – St. John the Apostle, 85

~ R ~

Radiologists – St. Michael the Archangel (Jan. 15, 1941), 85

Rape and Sexual Exploitation – St. Maria Goretti, 109

Refugees – St. Frances Xavier Cabrini, 109

Retreats – St. Ignatius Loyola (July 25, 1922), 35-36

Runaways and Missing Persons – Sts. Alodia and Nunilo, 110

Russia – St. Nicholas of Myra, St. Andrew, 129

~ S ~

Sacristans – St. Guy of Anderlecht, 36

Sailors – St. Brendan the Navigator, 85-86

Scandinavia – St. Ansgar, 130

Scholars – St. Bede the Venerable, 86-87

Scientists – St. Albert the Great (Aug. 13, 1948), 87

Scotland – St. Andrew the Apostle, p. xx; St. Columba, 130

Secretaries and Clerks – St. Genesius of Arles, 87-88

Seminarians – St. Charles Borromeo, 37

The Sick – St. Camillus de Lellis (June 22, 1886), 110

Single Men – St. Joseph Moscati, 52

Single Parents – St. Elizabeth Ann Seton, 52

Single Women – St. Margaret of Cortona, 52-53

Skaters – St. Lidwina of Schiedham, 88

Skiers – St. Bernard of Methon, 88

Slovakia – Our Lady of Sorrows, 130

Snake Protection – St. Patrick, 110

Social Workers – St. Louise de Marillac (Feb. 12, 1960), 89

Soldiers – St. Joan of Arc, 89-90

The Solomon Islands – The Most Holy Name of Mary (Sept. 4, 1991), 130-31

South Africa – Our Lady of the Assumption (March 15, 1952), 131

South America – St. Rose of Lima, 131

Spain – St. Teresa of Avila, St. James the Greater, 131

Sri Lanka – St. Lawrence, 132

Stepparents – St. (King) Leopold, 53

Storm Protection – St. Scholastica, 110
Stress – St. Walter of Pontnoise, 111
Students – St. Thomas Aquinas, 54, 90
Sweden – St. Bridget of Sweden, p. xx; St. Eric, 132
Swimmers – St. Adjutor, 90

~ T ~

Tanzania – The Immaculate Conception (Dec. 8, 1964), 132
Teachers – St. Jean Baptist de la Salle (May 15, 1950), 91
Telecommunications Workers – St. Gabriel the Archangel (Jan. 12, 1951),
    91
Television Writers and Television – St. Clare (Feb. 14, 1958), 91-92
Tertiaries or Third Order Members – St. Ferdinand III, 37-38
Theologians – St. Augustine, 38
Throat Ailments – St. Blaíse, 111
Toothaches – St. Apollonia, 111
Travelers – St. Christopher, 111

~ U ~

The United States – The Immaculate Conception (1846), 132-33
Uruguay – *La Virgen de los Treinte y Tres* (The Virgin of the Thirty-Three)
    (Nov. 21, 1963), 133-34

~ V ~

Venezuela – Our Lady of Coromoto, 133
Veterinarians – St. Blaíse, 92-93
Vietnam – Our Lady of La Vang – 134
Vocations – St. Alphonsus Liguori, 21-22
Volcano Protection – St. Agatha, 111

~ W ~

Wales – St. David of Wales, 134

Weather Dangers – St. Swithun, 112
West Indies – St. Gertrude the Great, 134-35
Widowers – St. Thomas More, 54
Widows – St. Jane Frances de Chantal, 54
Women in Labor – St. Anne, 112
Workers – St. Joseph, 93
Writers – St. Francis de Sales (April 26, 1923) 63

~ Y ~

Young Brides – St. Elizabeth of Hungary, 54
Young Women – St. Teresa of Jesus of the Andes, 55
Youth – St. Aloysius Gonzaga (1729 by Benedict XIII; 1926 by Pius XI), 55-56

Bibliography

Attwater, Donald, comp; Cumming, John, ed. *A New Dictionary of Saints*. Collegeville, Minn.: The Liturgical Press, 1993.

Attwater, Donald. *The Penguin Dictionary of Saints*. Middlesex, England: Penguin, 1965.

Bunson, Matthew, et al. *John Paul II's Book of Saints*. Huntington, Ind.: Our Sunday Visitor, 1999.

Bunson, Matthew, and Bunson, Margaret. *Lives of the Saints You Should Know* (vols. 1 and 2). Huntington, Ind.: Our Sunday Visitor, 1994.

Cruz, Joan Carroll. *Secular Saints: 250 Canonized and Beatified Lay Men, Women and Children*. Rockford, Ill.: TAN, 1989.

Chervin, Ronda De Sola. *Treasury of Women Saints*. Ann Arbor, Mich.: Servant Publications, 1991.

Freeze, Michael. *Patron Saints*. Huntington, Ind.: Our Sunday Visitor, 1992.

McBride, Alfred. *Saints Are People: Church History through the Saints*. Dubuque, Ia.: William C. Brown, 1981.

Newland, Mary Reed. *The Saint Book: For Parents, Teachers, Homilists, Storytellers, and Children*. New York: Seabury, 1979.

Our Sunday Visitor. *Our Sunday Visitor's Catholic Almanac, 2001*. Huntington, Ind.: Our Sunday Visitor, 2001.

Sandoval, Annette. *The Directory of Saints: A Concise Guide to Patron Saints*. New York: Penguin, 1997.

On-line Bibliographic Resources

Catholic Forum: Patron Saints Index (www.catholic-forum.com/saints)

University of Dayton, The Marian Library and International Marian Research Institute, "Marian Titles in the Popular Religiosity of Latin America," (translated from *"Las Advocaciones Marianas en la Religiosidad Popular Latinoamericana"*) (www.udayton.edu/mary/resources/english.html)